Instant Pot®
ITALIAN

Instant Pot®
ITALIAN

100 Irresistible Recipes Made Easier than Ever

Ivy Manning

Photography by Lauren Volo

Houghton Mifflin Harcourt
Boston • New York

Text copyright © 2018 by Ivy Manning

Photography copyright © 2018 by Lauren Volo

hmhco.com

Library of Congress Cataloging-in-Publication Data is available.

ISBN 978-1-328-46760-7 (pbk)

ISBN 978-1-328-46761-4 (ebk)

Book design by Tai Blanche

Food styling by Molly Shuster

Printed in the United States of America

DOC 10 9 8 7 6 5 4 3 2
4500700148

CONTENTS

RECIPES

INTRODUCTION

Close your eyes and imagine your favorite Italian food. You probably see a pot on the stove burbling away for hours, filling the kitchen with the wonderful aroma of tomatoes, garlic, and oregano. Perhaps there's a scattering of antipasti dishes on the table, alongside golden brown crostini. Maybe it's a big bowl of pasta, a long-simmered osso buco on creamy risotto, or hearty chicken cacciatore. If you have a sweet tooth, an espresso chocolate cake or creamy Sicilian *cassata* might come to mind, too.

At first blush, it may seem unlikely that a modern appliance like the Instant Pot could tackle all these diverse dishes successfully. I'm here to tell you the good news: The Instant Pot can cook all these things, better and faster than traditional methods.

In this book, I've tapped into my experience cooking and living in Italy to translate my favorite Italian dishes to the Instant Pot. Although the Instant Pot has several functions, including "Slow Cook," "Rice," and "Steam," I've found that the "Sauté" function and the manual "Pressure Cook" function do just about everything you need to make incredible Italian food.

Since your time is valuable, I include the real time it takes to make each recipe, both the hands-on preparation time and the total time, which includes the time it takes the pot to come up to pressure and for the pressure to release, so you can plan efficiently. You'll find that there are often time-saving instructions so you can multitask as the cooking gets under way,

and notes on recipes that store well or are good do-ahead candidates. One-pot meals—easy to make and a boon to those who hate washing too many pots and pans—are denoted with an icon.

Italians start meals with antipasti, so this book begins with a chapter full of recipes like eggplant caponata, tender seafood and grain salads, deviled eggs, and even focaccia to start your meal. The Instant Pot makes these dishes so easy, you'll be able to serve a fancy-looking first course when entertaining, a quick nibble to serve with cocktails, or a light lunch in minutes.

Next you'll find favorite soups like Minestrone, Tuscan Beef Stew, and Cannellini and Kale, plus some regional Italian soups you may not be familiar with that will add diverse flavors to your repertoire. Cooking soups under pressure not only makes beans, grains, and meats tender in minutes, it also super-charges the flavors. You may never use your old soup pot again!

In the chapter on pasta and grains, I share the sauces I learned during kitchen stints in Italy, adapted specifically for the Instant Pot. Cooking under pressure not only intensifies the flavors of tomatoes and aromatics, it also breaks down short ribs, veggies, and even lamb into hearty ragùs that would make an Italian grand-mother proud.

Pasta sauces in the Instant Pot are a no-brainer, but did you know that you can cook an entire pasta dish all at once, dry noodles and all? It's so exciting to drop dry penne, cherry tomatoes, olives, broth, and a fresh tuna steak into the pot, press a button, and come back to a restaurant-worthy meal! Speaking of Italian restaurants, this chapter also shows you how to use your Instant Pot to make remarkably creamy risotto and polenta, no constant stirring required.

In the chapter on pork, beef, and lamb, I've adapted the beautiful, thrifty braised meat dishes that Italian cuisine is known for. The Instant Pot makes amazing Milanese osso buco, Tuscan milk-braised pork loin, and lamb shanks that melt in your mouth. In addition to authentic meat dishes from Italy, I couldn't help but add some of my favorite Italian-American dishes, like Chicago sliced beef sandwiches, pork chops with figs, and gooey mozzarella-stuffed meatballs in marinara.

Chicken is a go-to for Italian and American cooks alike. In the poultry chapter, I'll introduce you to the wonders of classic dishes like chicken cacciatore, ground turkey–stuffed bell peppers, and braised duck ragù from Venice. If you've heard that chicken breasts are a no-go in the intense heat of the Instant Pot, my foolproof recipes for juicy chicken breasts stuffed with fresh mozzarella, tomatoes, and basil and chicken breasts braised in sweet bell pepper *peperonata* will change your mind.

You might be so enamored with what the Instant Pot can do for soup, pasta, and meat recipes that you forget your veggies, but you definitely shouldn't. I

have a whole chapter devoted to them, and I'll show you the keys to using the Instant Pot to cook hard vegetables (think baby artichokes, celery root, and winter squash) in a fraction of the time they'd require on the stove. I'll also show you how to cook tender vegetables Italian style—tomato-braised green beans, broccoli rabe with peppers, and even a clever riff on eggplant Parmesan. You'll see that the Instant Pot can be a handy tool to create tasty side dishes without taking up valuable stove space or requiring much work.

You've no doubt already heard the wonders of cooking cheesecakes in the Instant Pot, but that's not all the machine can do for dessert. I've converted my favorite Italian desserts to Instant Pot cooking, including miraculously moist cakes, silky custards, and even a molten-center espresso-chocolate number.

In the final chapter, I share reliable recipes for homemade pantry items that are the backbone of great Italian cooking. There are lessons on how to cook perfectly plump beans, essential homemade broths, and a delicious homemade marinara sauce that's leagues above the jarred stuff. You can even make homemade ricotta using your Instant Pot's "Yogurt" setting!

Armed with this book and your Instant Pot multi-cooker, you'll grow your repertoire of Italian cooking and get dinner on the table with minimal fuss. *Mangia, mangia!*

TEN TIPS FOR BETTER ITALIAN INSTANT POT DISHES

These tenets are applicable to any cuisine, but they're especially true for authentic Italian flavor.

1. QUALITY IN, QUALITY OUT

Italian cooks know that the best dishes use the best ingredients—keep it simple, and let the flavors shine. There aren't a lot of special ingredients called for in this book, but you do want to use good-quality ones to up your Italian cooking game. (No green-can "Parmesan," please!) See Must-Have Ingredients (page 19) for some of my favorites.

2. GET THE POT HOT

You may be tempted to press "Sauté" and add everything all at once, but if you add meat to a cold pot, it will stick, and vegetables will sweat instead of brown. Get into the habit of pressing Sauté first thing, and the Instant Pot will beep and let you know when it's hot enough to get cooking. While the pot heats up, prepare the ingredients.

3. FRESH HERBS ARE BETTER

I recommend using fresh herbs (and lots of them) in most of the recipes in this book. Since Instant Pot recipes cook quickly, fresh herbs, which release their flavor faster, are best. I've included dried herbs as an alternative in most recipes, but I do recommend using fresh.

4. DON'T COOK WITH WINE YOU WOULDN'T DRINK

This is especially important when using an Instant Pot because the wine won't evaporate as much, so harsh-tasting wine has nowhere to hide. You'll never need more than 1 cup for cooking any recipe—the rest is to drink with dinner.

5. DON'T DROWN THE DISH

Yes, you need liquid to build up steam in the Instant Pot and bring the pot to pressure, but most novices end up adding too much liquid, which dilutes flavor. In most cases, ½ to 1 cup broth or other liquid (including crushed tomatoes) is enough. Keep in mind that many ingredients add plenty of their own moisture as they cook. Follow these recipes, which have been rigorously tested, and you'll never have to worry about adding the wrong amount of liquid.

6. USE FLAVORFUL LIQUIDS

With conventional stovetop cooking, about 30 percent of the liquid in a recipe will evaporate as you simmer it. In the sealed environment of the Instant Pot, just 3 to 5 percent of the liquid will evaporate. That's why it's important that the liquids you add to a soup or braise are good and flavorful. Water will add moisture but not flavor; in most cases, I prefer broth, and that's what I call for in the recipes. Homemade is best—and fortunately, it's also a breeze to make in the Instant Pot (see pages 198–201).

7. DOUBLE-CHECK THE SEALING RING

I've cooked hundreds of meals in the Instant Pot, but every once in a while, I still forget to fit the sealing ring into the lid. It's only after several minutes, when the pot doesn't come up to pressure, that I realize my mistake. Get in the habit of checking to make sure the sealing ring is in place every time you use your Instant Pot.

8. DON'T RUSH THE RELEASE

In recipes where there's no danger of food overcooking, I recommend letting the pressure in the pot come down naturally for at least 10 to 15 minutes (this is noted in the recipes where applicable). This gentle pressure release helps to keep foods like beans intact, and for meats, it's similar to resting a roast on a cutting board before slicing it—the extra time allows the juices to evenly redistribute throughout the meat

so it's extra juicy and won't shred when sliced. On the other hand, the quick-release method is ideal for fast-cooking things like white meat chicken and tender vegetables; the intense heat of the quick-release method is factored into the timing of these recipes.

9. THICKEN AT THE END

Because there is no evaporation in the closed Instant Pot pressure cooking system, sauces won't reduce as they would in traditional Italian recipes. That means in some recipes, you'll need to thicken the sauce a little at the end. My favorite thickening agent for the Instant Pot is *beurre manié*, a flour-butter mixture similar to roux that's whisked into sauces at the end of cooking. For especially rich sauces that don't need extra butter, I use a cornstarch slurry instead. You can also use the "Sauté" function once the lid is off to simmer and reduce a sauce before serving.

10. GET TO KNOW YOUR "KEEP WARM" BUTTON

Most of the time, you want the "Keep Warm" function turned off to prevent overcooking. On older models of the Instant Pot (Duo Version 1 and Lux models), the "Keep Warm" function automatically turns on when the pressure cooking function is done. You've got to be there to press the button at the end of the pressure cooking cycle if you want to turn it off. On the updated Duo Version 2, you can press the "Keep Warm" button twice before the cooking program starts to turn off this function. On the Duo Plus and more recent models, simply press the "Keep Warm" button once before the cooking program starts; the yellow light on the button will turn off, indicating that the function is disengaged.

QUICK SAFETY REMINDERS

If you haven't already, read the manual that came with your Instant Pot and familiarize yourself with the safety guidelines. Here are a few quick reminders and tips for using your appliance safely and effectively.

Set up your Instant Pot under the venting hood on your stove. When you release steam from the venting valve, you're shooting hot, moist air into your kitchen (and at the kitchen wall). I recommend placing your Instant Pot on a baking sheet on the stove and turning the stove's venting hood on high to suck up odors and smoke when sautéing and to dissipate steam when releasing pressure from the venting valve.

Never overfill the Instant Pot. Never fill the inner pot more than two-thirds full with liquid. When cooking a chicken or roast, it's okay if the solid portion of the ingredients is above the two-thirds line. When cooking ingredients that expand or foam when cooking (beans, pasta, grains), don't fill the pot more than halfway. The recipes in this book take this into account.

Stand by until the pressure comes up. The Instant Pot is a "set it and forget it" appliance, but it's a good idea to keep an eye on it while the pot comes up to pressure just to make sure everything is working properly. Once the pressure cooking cycle has started (it will beep and display the time remaining), it's fine to walk away and go about your day.

Keep your distance when releasing the pressure through the venting valve. Use a long-handled spoon to move the venting valve to "Venting." Hot steam will come out of the valve quickly and rather forcefully, so it's best to keep your distance.

When two-step cooking, cool the lid and sealing ring before resealing the pot. If you are following a two-step recipe where you stop the pressure cooking, add an ingredient, and bring the pot back up to pressure, you may have difficulty locking the hot lid back on the machine. This is because the silicone sealing ring in the lid expands as it warms up. If you're having trouble resealing the lid, rinse the lid and ring under cool running water. Once the lid and ring cool down, it will be easier to lock on the lid and proceed.

Tilt the lid away from you when opening the pot. Steam and condensation are trapped under the Instant Pot lid, so remember to wear an oven mitt and open the lid away from you when you unlock the lid. Don't let condensation on the inside of the lid drip back into the pot—especially important when making casseroles and cakes that aren't covered with foil.

Monitor the state of the sealing ring. The sealing ring that sits tightly in the lid should be springy with no cracks. Depending on how much you use your Instant Pot, a silicone sealing ring should last for several months. I recommend having a few extras on hand, including one that is set aside for use with dessert recipes only. They're inexpensive and readily available online.

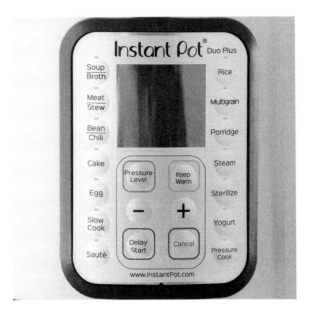

There are handy pre-set buttons on the control panel. For this book, you'll be using the Sauté, Pressure Cook, and Pressure Level buttons most frequently.

Use a wooden spoon to switch the valve to the "Venting" position in order to safely release steam.

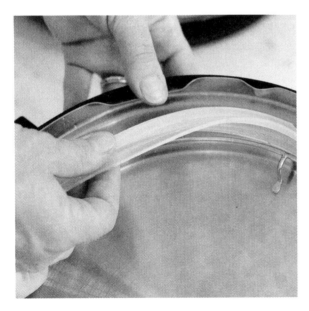

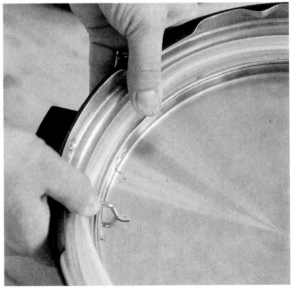

Monitor the sealing ring for cracks. Replace it if rigid or cracked.

Make sure the sealing ring is fitted snugly into the lid before placing the lid on the Instant Pot.

MUST-HAVE INGREDIENTS

PARMESAN

When I list "Parmesan cheese" in the ingredients list, I mean real Parmigiano-Reggiano cheese. The aged Italian cheese has a dry, crumbly texture and nutty, umami-rich flavor that no other cheese can come close to. It's fine to buy pre-grated Parmigiano-Reggiano for convenience, but steer clear of "Italian" cheese blends; they're often full of cheap domestic substitutes. Many recipes in this book call for a Parmesan cheese rind. These rock-hard rinds infuse sauces and soups with extra flavor and are discarded at the end, as you would a bay leaf. Start saving your Parmesan rinds and bank them for later; they keep for months in the refrigerator.

OLIVE OIL

When I call for olive oil in a recipe, I mean extra-virgin olive oil—it's the best quality and the best-tasting. Regular olive oil or olive oil blends are made with the cheapest olives available and often have off-flavors. I use so much extra-virgin olive oil that I buy it in large metal half-gallon tins: It's much less expensive than bottled, and the oil keeps well for months in the cool, dark pantry. The big tin is a bit unwieldly, so I pour only what I'll use in a week or so into an attractive smaller bottle for easy pouring when I'm cooking.

CANNED TOMATOES

Scores of recipes in this book call for canned tomatoes.

For **whole tomatoes**, I recommend buying San Marzano DOP (Protected Designation of Origin) tomatoes. They're imported from Italy and are carefully grown, packed, and monitored for quality. There are also "San Marzano–style" canned tomatoes, essentially San Marzano heirloom varietals grown domestically, which are also fine; just know that they vary in flavor and quality from brand to brand. It's a good idea to always keep a few cans on hand in your pantry.

For **crushed tomatoes**, which are essentially whole tomatoes crushed to a fairly smooth texture, I like the bright, sweet flavor of Cento brand. If you're feeling ambitious or you only have whole tomatoes on hand, you can make your own crushed tomatoes by running whole canned tomatoes and their juice through a food mill.

I call for **boxed or canned diced tomatoes in puree** in a few recipes. These tomatoes are diced and treated with calcium chloride, a natural food additive that helps the tomato pieces keep their shape. They are ideal for soups and some braises when you want to retain the texture of the tomatoes. I use Pomi chopped tomatoes, which come in a handy aseptic box.

DRIED PORCINI MUSHROOMS

These are prized in Italy for their intense, earthy flavor. Look for packages of large, smooth (not wrinkled) sliced porcini mushrooms at gourmet stores, better grocery stores, and Italian markets. I order them online from The Spice House (thespicehouse.com). It's best to either rinse or soak the mushrooms (the correct method is specified in each recipe) to remove grit before adding them to a recipe.

PANCETTA

This is salt and pepper–cured pork belly used in Italian cooking to add a little meaty punch and richness. For the best texture, I recommend buying pre-diced pancetta or buying a ½-inch-thick slice from a deli and dicing it into ¼-inch cubes. Don't buy thinly sliced pancetta; it will just disappear into dishes. Unsmoked, uncured, thick-cut pepper bacon is a reasonable substitute.

VERMOUTH

When I need a little dry white wine to deglaze the pot, I'll often grab a bottle of dry vermouth to do the job instead. The neutral, slightly herbal notes and bone-dry character of dry white vermouth plays nicely with most foods. It also comes in handy screw-top bottles and keeps for months in the refrigerator, nice if you don't feel like opening a bottle of wine just for cooking. I like California-made Vya vermouth.

ANTIPASTI AND SALADS

Long, leisurely meals with multiple courses and pre-dinner nibbling are a key part of Italian life. The spreads, salads, and appetizers that start the meal are collectively known as *antipasti*.

Classic spreads like eggplant caponata, creamy salt cod mousse, and chicken liver pâté are perfect candidates for the Instant Pot because pressure cooking makes the ingredients tender and locks in their flavorful moisture. As are hearty Italian salads, because dense ingredients like beans, whole grains, beets, and potatoes cook quickly to tender perfection.

Other recipes in this chapter showcase the Instant Pot's incredible versatility: perfect hard-boiled eggs that are remarkably easy to peel, for "Italianified" deviled eggs; a quick giardiniera pickle; and even rosemary-flecked olive oil bread. Bread in the Instant Pot? *Per certo!*

CAPONATA

Serves 6 Active time: 15 minutes Total time: 50 minutes

The eggplant, bell peppers, currants, and spices in this famous Sicilian vegetable dish
are transformed into an incredibly rich, savory combination when cooked under pressure
for just 4 minutes. Serve this spread mounded on top of crostini made from Homemade
Focaccia (page 31), or as a condiment for grilled lamb or chicken. I've even been
known to toss the mixture with cooked pasta for an impromptu summer pasta salad.

1 large (1-pound) eggplant,
  cut into 1-inch cubes

  Salt and pepper

3 tablespoons olive oil

1 medium red onion,
  chopped

1 red bell pepper, chopped

1 teaspoon dried oregano

3 garlic cloves, thinly sliced

1 cup crushed tomatoes

3 tablespoons
  balsamic vinegar

3 tablespoons dried currants
  or raisins

1 teaspoon unsweetened
  cocoa powder

1 teaspoon sugar

½ teaspoon
  ground cinnamon

3 tablespoons pine nuts,
  toasted

1 Toss the eggplant with 1 teaspoon salt in a colander and set aside for
30 minutes; this extracts some of the eggplant's bitter juices. Pat the
eggplant dry with paper towels.

2 Put the oil in the pot, select **SAUTÉ**, and adjust to **MORE/HIGH** heat.
When the oil is hot, add the onion, bell pepper, and oregano and cook,
stirring occasionally, until just tender, 5 minutes. Press **CANCEL**.

3 Add the eggplant and remaining ingredients except the pine nuts and
stir to combine. Lock on the lid, select the **PRESSURE COOK** function,
and adjust to **HIGH** pressure for 4 minutes. Make sure the steam valve is in
the "Sealing" position and that the "Keep Warm" button is off.

4 When the cooking time is up, quick-release the pressure. Season with
salt and black pepper. Transfer the caponata to a serving bowl and let
it stand until room temperature. Stir in the pine nuts just before serving.

*The caponata can be stored in the refrigerator in an airtight container for up to
5 days. Bring to room temperature before serving.*

CREAMY SALT COD SPREAD

Serves 6 to 8 | Active time: 15 minutes | Total time: 45 minutes

Baccalà mantecato, or "whipped salt cod" in Italian, is a creamy, savory mousse made from salt cod, potatoes, and copious amounts of good extra-virgin olive oil. Look for the cute wooden boxes of salt cod at grocery stores with good seafood departments; it's often frozen. To prepare the cod, you'll need to soak it in the refrigerator for 48 hours, changing the water a few times, before proceeding with the recipe. Serve the *baccalà* with toasted crostini or grilled bruschetta.

8 ounces salt cod

2 lemon slices

4 medium garlic cloves, peeled and left whole

3 sprigs fresh thyme

1 medium (8-ounce) russet potato, peeled and halved lengthwise

2 tablespoons fresh lemon juice

⅓ cup olive oil

Salt and pepper

1 tablespoon finely chopped fresh Italian parsley

Crostini or bruschetta, for serving

1 Soak the cod in a large bowl of cold water in the refrigerator for 48 hours, changing the water at least twice a day. To test if the fish is ready, break off a little piece and taste it; it should be briny but not chokingly salty. When the fish is edible, drain well and pat dry.

2 Place the lemon slices, garlic, and thyme sprigs in the bottom of the pot and add 3 cups cold water. Place the cod in the pot. Place a trivet in the pot over the fish and place the potato halves on top. Lock on the lid, select the **PRESSURE COOK** function, and adjust to **HIGH** pressure for 10 minutes. Make sure the steam valve is in the "Sealing" position and that the "Keep Warm" button is off.

3 When the cooking time is up, quick-release the pressure. Remove the potatoes, cod, and garlic cloves from the pot with a slotted spoon; reserve 2 tablespoons of the cooking water and discard the rest.

4 Transfer the cod, lemon juice, and reserved cooking water to a food processor and process until finely chopped. With the machine running, slowly add the olive oil through the feed tube.

5 In a medium bowl, mash the potatoes with a masher until smooth. Add the cod mixture and beat with a wooden spoon until fluffy, 2 minutes. Season with salt and pepper. Garnish with the parsley and serve at room temperature, on crostini or bruschetta.

The spread can be stored in an airtight container in the refrigerator for up to 4 days. Let it come to room temperature or reheat to room temperature in the microwave before serving.

TUSCAN CHICKEN LIVER PÂTÉ

Serves 8 | Active time: 25 minutes | Total time: 1 hour 30 minutes, plus 6 hours marinating time

I learned to make this chicken liver mousse twenty-five years ago while studying abroad in Florence, Italy. Though the ingredients remain the same, I've found that cooking the ingredients in the Instant Pot yields an especially smooth pâté that is delicious spread on toasted slices of Rosemary Focaccia (page 31) or rustic bread. The pâté thickens as it cools, so allow at least 1 hour of chilling time.

10 ounces chicken livers

1 cup whole or 2% milk

2 tablespoons olive oil

1 small shallot, finely chopped

1 small carrot, finely chopped

1 celery rib, finely chopped

Generous pinch of ground allspice

Salt and pepper

¼ cup Marsala wine or dry vermouth

½ cup Homemade Chicken Broth (page 198) or low-sodium store-bought broth

2 tablespoons heavy cream

1 teaspoon finely grated lemon zest

2 tablespoons finely chopped fresh Italian parsley

1 Rinse the livers in cold water, drain, and place in a medium bowl. Pour the milk over the livers, cover with plastic, and refrigerate for at least 6 hours and up to 24 hours; this will help remove any impurities and improve the flavor of the pâté.

2 Drain the livers and discard the milk. Pat the livers dry with paper towels and set aside. Put the oil in the pot, select **SAUTÉ**, and adjust to **NORMAL/MEDIUM** heat. When the oil is hot, add the shallot, carrot, and celery and cook, stirring frequently, until tender, 4 minutes.

3 Push the vegetables aside in the pot and add the chicken livers, allspice, a few pinches of salt, and a few grinds of pepper. Cook the livers until lightly colored, about 1 minute per side. Add the wine and cook for 1 minute to burn off some of the alcohol. Press **CANCEL**.

4 Add the broth to the pot. Lock on the lid, select the **PRESSURE COOK** function, and adjust to **HIGH** pressure for 3 minutes. Make sure the steam valve is in the "Sealing" position and that the "Keep Warm" button is off.

5 When the cooking time is up, quick-release the pressure. Add the cream and lemon zest to the pot. Use an immersion blender to blend the mixture until smooth. (Alternatively, carefully transfer the mixture to a blender and blend with the lid slightly ajar to allow steam to escape.) Using a rubber spatula, push the pâté through a fine-mesh sieve into a bowl; discard the solids. Refrigerate the pâté, uncovered, for at least 1 hour before serving, garnished with the parsley.

The pâté can be stored in an airtight container in the refrigerator for up to 3 days.

AUTUMN FRUIT MOSTARDA

Makes 2½ cups; serves 12 Active time: 10 minutes Total time: 35 minutes

Mostarda is an Italian fruit chutney served as a condiment alongside creamy cheeses and rich roasted meats. Traditional recipes require lots of slow simmering of the fruit and spices, but the Instant Pot cuts the enterprise down to just over half an hour. *Mostarda*, as the name suggests, includes a bit of powdered mustard, but if you'd prefer to leave it out, by all means do so.

2 large (8-ounce) firm Bosc pears, peeled, cored, and cut into 1-inch chunks

1 large (8-ounce) tart green apple, peeled, cored, and cut into 1-inch chunks

½ cup dried figs (4 ounces), snipped into small pieces with scissors

⅓ cup dried apricots (4 ounces), snipped into small pieces with scissors

½ cup sugar

½ cup white balsamic or white wine vinegar

2 (4-inch-long) strips orange zest, peeled with a vegetable peeler

2 whole cloves

Pinch of salt

1 tablespoon mustard powder

1 Combine the pears, apple, figs, apricots, sugar, vinegar, orange zest, cloves, and salt in the pot. Lock on the lid, select the **PRESSURE COOK** function, and adjust to **HIGH** pressure for 5 minutes. Make sure the steam valve is in the "Sealing" position and that the "Keep Warm" button is off.

2 When the cooking time is up, let the pressure come down naturally for 10 minutes and then quick-release the remaining pressure. Using a slotted spoon, transfer the fruit to a nonreactive airtight container or jar.

3 Whisk the mustard powder into the juices in the pot and ladle the mixture over the fruit in the container. Refrigerate, uncovered, until completely cool before serving.

The mostarda can be stored in an airtight container in the refrigerator for up to 2 weeks or in the freezer for up to 3 months.

MARINATED BEET SALAD WITH GORGONZOLA AND HAZELNUTS

Serves 4 | Active time: 10 minutes | Total time: 30 minutes

Beets steam in just 15 minutes in the Instant Pot and the skins slip off easily once they're cool enough to handle, so you can have beets in minutes instead of the hour that oven roasting requires. Whole garlic cloves steam alongside the beets and make a creamy, flavorful base for the dressing. Make sure to buy like-sized beets so they cook evenly.

3   medium (5-ounce) beets without tops

3   large garlic cloves, unpeeled and left whole

1   medium shallot, finely chopped

2   tablespoons balsamic vinegar

2   tablespoons olive oil

2   tablespoons dried currants

1   tablespoon chopped fresh marjoram or oregano leaves

Salt and pepper

2   cups arugula or mixed baby greens

½   cup Gorgonzola dolce cheese (2½ ounces)

¼   cup chopped toasted hazelnuts

1 Place a steamer basket in the bottom of the pot and pour in 1½ cups cold water. Place the beets and garlic in the steamer. Lock on the lid, select the **PRESSURE COOK** function, and adjust to **HIGH** pressure for 15 minutes.

2 In a large bowl, whisk together the shallot, vinegar, oil, currants, marjoram, and 1 teaspoon salt; set aside.

3 When the cooking time is up, quick-release the pressure. The beets are done when a paring knife slides easily into the center of the largest beet. If the beets are still hard, cook them on **HIGH** pressure for 1 minute more, then quick-release the pressure.

4 Transfer the beets and garlic to a plate. When cool enough to handle, peel the garlic, add to the bowl with the shallot mixture, and whisk to combine. Slide the peels off the beets with your fingers and discard the skins. Cut the beets into bite-size pieces and add them to the bowl. Season with salt and pepper and toss to coat.

5 Mound the greens on plates. Top the greens with the beets, dabs of the cheese, and the nuts. Serve warm or at room temperature.

The cooled beets and garlic can be stored in an airtight container in the refrigerator for up to 5 days. Bring to room temperature before assembling the salad.

ROSEMARY FOCACCIA

Serves 8 | Active time: 15 minutes | Total time: 1 hour 15 minutes

Bread in the Instant Pot? You bet! This delicious rosemary and olive oil loaf proofs in the moist environment of the Instant Pot and then steam-bakes under pressure in just 20 minutes. Because there is no browning, it won't look like the golden brown focaccia from your favorite bakery, but the loaf makes excellent crostini or bruschetta once sliced and toasted or grilled. Omit the rosemary if you'd prefer plain focaccia.

¾ cup warm water

1½ teaspoons honey

2¼ teaspoons active dry yeast

2½ tablespoons olive oil

1 tablespoon chopped fresh rosemary

2 cups all-purpose flour, plus more for dusting

¾ teaspoon salt

1 In a large bowl, combine the water, honey, and yeast and stir to dissolve. Let the mixture stand at room temperature until foamy, 5 minutes. Add 1 tablespoon of the oil and the rosemary and stir to combine. Add the flour and salt and stir with a wooden spoon until the mixture forms a sticky ball, about 1 minute. Transfer the dough to a lightly floured surface and knead until smooth and elastic, about 8 minutes. (Alternatively, mix the ingredients in the bowl of a stand mixer with the dough hook on medium speed for 4 minutes.)

2 Place a trivet in the pot and pour in 1½ cups hot water. Brush an 8-inch round pan that will fit into the Instant Pot with 1 tablespoon of the oil. Transfer the dough to the pan and spread it out with your fingers to cover the bottom of the pan. Cover the pan loosely with plastic wrap and place it on the trivet in the pot. Cover the pot with a regular pan lid and let the dough rise for at least 30 minutes and up to 1 hour. (Do not turn on the Instant Pot.)

3 Take the pan out of the pot and discard the plastic. Brush a piece of foil with the remaining ½ tablespoon oil and cover the pan with it, sealing the edges tightly. Set the pan on the trivet. Lock on the lid, select the **PRESSURE COOK** function, and adjust to **HIGH** pressure for 20 minutes. Make sure the steam valve is in the "Sealing" position and that the "Keep Warm" button is off.

4 When the cooking time is up, let the pressure come down naturally for 10 minutes and then quick-release the remaining pressure. Blot the top of the foil with paper towels to remove any condensation. Remove the pan from the pot, discard the foil, and let the bread cool for 10 minutes. Run a knife around the edges of the pan and invert the pan to remove the bread.

The bread can be kept at room temperature, tightly wrapped, for up to 4 days.

FARRO, PEAR, AND WALNUT SALAD

Serves 4   Active time: 10 minutes   Total time: 50 minutes

Farro is an ancient grain related to wheat that is used in salads, soups, and even desserts in Italy. I use whole-grain farro, as opposed to pearled farro, in salads like this because the grains retain a plump texture that "pops" in your mouth when chewed. Pears and walnuts add sweetness and crunch to this salad, while aged Gorgonzola piccante (look for it at well-stocked supermarkets or specialty cheese shops) adds a salty hit. If you can't find piccante Gorgonzola, use your favorite crumbly blue cheese.

¾   cup whole-grain farro

3   tablespoons olive oil

1   bay leaf

    Salt and pepper

2   tablespoons apple cider vinegar

1   tablespoon honey

1   medium Bosc pear, cored and chopped

⅓   cup crumbled Gorgonzola piccante cheese (2 ounces)

½   cup walnuts, toasted and coarsely chopped

3   cups loosely packed baby arugula

1. Combine the farro, 2 cups cold water, 1 tablespoon of the oil, the bay leaf, and 1 teaspoon salt in the pot. Lock on the lid, select the **PRESSURE COOK** function, and adjust to **HIGH** pressure for 20 minutes. Make sure the steam valve is in the "Sealing" position and that the "Keep Warm" button is off.

2. When the cooking time is up, let the pressure come down naturally for 10 minutes and then quick-release the remaining pressure. Drain the farro and put it in a large serving bowl. In a small jar, combine the remaining 2 tablespoons oil, the vinegar, honey, and a few grinds of pepper. Screw on the lid and shake until the honey has dissolved. Toss the farro with the dressing and let cool for 10 minutes.

3. Add the pears, cheese, and walnuts to the farro and season with salt and pepper. Mound the arugula on top of the salad and serve.

The farro can be cooked, cooled, and stored in an airtight container in the refrigerator for up to 5 days, or in the freezer for up to 3 months. Defrost before using.

ANTIPASTO SALAD

Serves 4 to 6   Active time: 15 minutes   Total time: 45 minutes

Here are all the best ingredients from an antipasto platter, tossed together into a delicious salad that just begs to be taken on a picnic. Cooking the garbanzo beans with onions, fresh oregano, and dehydrated tomatoes in the Instant Pot yields beans that are infused with flavor. Then it's just a matter of tossing them with fresh mozzarella, salami, and olives. Serve with crostini or on a bed of baby arugula.

3 tablespoons olive oil

½ medium red onion, chopped

2 teaspoons chopped fresh oregano, or 1 teaspoon dried

3 medium garlic cloves, chopped

2 cups soaked garbanzo beans (from 1 cup dried beans; see page 196)

¼ cup dehydrated (sun-dried; not oil-packed) tomatoes

Salt and pepper

3 ounces ciliegine (bite-size fresh mozzarella balls), halved

½ cup pitted black olives, halved

½ cup chopped jarred roasted red peppers

1 (3-ounce) chunk salami, cut into ¼-inch cubes (about ½ cup)

1 tablespoon red wine vinegar

1 Put 2 tablespoons of the oil in the pot, select **SAUTÉ**, and adjust to **NORMAL/MEDIUM** heat. When the oil is hot, add the onion and oregano and cook, stirring frequently, until the onion is tender, 4 minutes. Add the garlic and cook until fragrant, 45 seconds.

2 Drain the garbanzo beans and add them to the pot along with 2 cups cold water, the dehydrated tomatoes, 1¼ teaspoons salt, and several grinds of black pepper. Lock on the lid, select the **PRESSURE COOK** function, and adjust to **HIGH** pressure for 2 minutes. Make sure the steam valve is in the "Sealing" position and that the "Keep Warm" button is off.

3 When the cooking time is up, let the pressure come down naturally, about 15 minutes. Drain the beans, place them in a large serving bowl, and let cool for a few minutes.

4 Add the remaining 1 tablespoon oil, the cheese, olives, roasted peppers, salami, and vinegar and toss to combine. Season with salt and black pepper. Serve at room temperature.

The salad can be stored in an airtight container in the refrigerator for up to 3 days. Bring to room temperature before serving.

CANNELLINI BEAN, FENNEL, AND TUNA SALAD

Serves 4 to 6 **Active time: 10 minutes** **Total time: 10 minutes**

This protein-packed salad is the perfect dish for an al fresco lunch, but it could also be served as part of an antipasto spread. Because it's so simple, every detail matters. That's why it's so important to use homemade pressure-cooked cannellini beans (they really do taste better!), quality olive oil–packed tuna, and good extra-virgin olive oil.

1 small (8-ounce) fennel bulb, stalks removed

¼ small red onion

2 cups Pressure-Cooked Cannellini Beans (page 197)

1 (5-ounce) can tuna packed in oil (such as Ortiz brand), broken up with a fork

¼ cup finely chopped fresh Italian parsley

3 tablespoons fresh lemon juice

3 tablespoons extra-virgin olive oil

1 tablespoon white wine vinegar

1 medium garlic clove, minced

Salt and pepper

1 Cut the fennel and onion into thin slices using a mandoline or sharp chef's knife. Place the vegetables in a large serving bowl. Add the beans, tuna, and parsley.

2 In a small jar, combine the lemon juice, oil, vinegar, and garlic. Screw on the lid and shake vigorously. Pour the dressing over the salad. Season generously with salt and pepper and toss gently to combine.

CORONA BEANS WITH TOMATO AND SAGE

Serves 6 as an appetizer or 4 as a side dish   Active time: 10 minutes
Total time: 1 hour 20 minutes, plus soaking time

Corona beans are large white beans with creamy centers that are often served as a cold appetizer in Italy. They are also great warm as a side dish for grilled sausages or other meats. Look for dry corona beans (sometimes labeled "gigante beans") at natural foods stores and Italian groceries. To ensure that the finished beans are tender with intact skins, soak the beans for just 6 hours before cooking them; any longer and they tend to germinate and become tough.

8   ounces dried corona (gigante) beans (1½ cups)

2   tablespoons olive oil

½   medium yellow onion, finely chopped

1   tablespoon finely chopped fresh sage leaves, or 1½ teaspoons dried

3   medium garlic cloves, chopped

     Salt and pepper

1   bay leaf

½   cup boxed or canned diced tomatoes in puree

1   Pick over the beans and toss out any rocks or shriveled beans. Rinse the beans with cold water and place them in a large bowl. Add enough cold water to cover them by 3 inches. Soak the beans at room temperature for 6 hours. Drain.

2   Put the oil in the pot, select **SAUTÉ**, and adjust to **NORMAL/MEDIUM** heat. When the oil is hot, add the onions and sage and cook, stirring frequently, until the onion is tender, 4 minutes. Add the garlic and cook until fragrant, 45 seconds. Press **CANCEL**.

3   Add the soaked beans to the pot along with 2 cups cold water, 1 teaspoon salt, a few grinds of pepper, and the bay leaf. Lock on the lid, select the **PRESSURE COOK** function, and adjust to **HIGH** pressure for 25 minutes. Make sure the steam valve is in the "Sealing" position and that the "Keep Warm" button is off.

4   When the cooking time is up, let the pressure come down naturally; this will take about 20 minutes. Test a bean; it should be creamy in the center. If the beans are not done, place a regular pan lid on the pot, select **SAUTÉ**, adjust to **NORMAL/MEDIUM**, and simmer until tender.

5   Remove the lid, ladle off and discard ½ cup of the cooking liquid, and discard the bay leaf. There may be a few corona beans floating on top of the cooking liquid that remain hard and opaque; if so, discard them.

(recipe continues)

(continued from page 36)

6 Add the tomatoes to the pot, select **SAUTÉ**, and adjust to **NORMAL/ MEDIUM** heat. Simmer the beans, uncovered, stirring gently with a rubber spatula, until the sauce has thickened a little, 5 minutes. Season with salt and pepper. Press **CANCEL**. Transfer the beans to a serving bowl and let stand at room temperature for at least 10 minutes so the beans can absorb some of the cooking liquid. Serve warm or at room temperature.

The beans can be stored in the refrigerator in an airtight container for up to 5 days. Reheat or bring to room temperature before serving.

SQUID, TOMATO, AND OLIVE SALAD

Serves 4   Active time: 15 minutes   Total time: 1 hour

If you've always been afraid to cook calamari because you thought it'd be rubbery, this recipe will change your mind. The Instant Pot makes squid incredibly tender. In this recipe, cooked squid is tossed with heirloom tomatoes, olives, and parsley for a simple salad that's perfect for the dog days of summer. If you've never bought squid before, don't worry—it's often sold already cleaned, or the fishmonger at the counter can do it for you. This recipe can be made more substantial by adding 3 cups of cooked shell pasta (6 ounces dried, before cooking) to the mix at the end; increase the olive oil to taste.

½ cup dry vermouth or dry white wine

4 medium garlic cloves, finely chopped

1 tablespoon chopped fresh oregano, or 1 teaspoon dried

10 whole black peppercorns

2 pounds cleaned squid bodies and tentacles

1 cup Homemade Seafood Broth (page 200) or canned clam juice

1 large (12-ounce) heirloom tomato, chopped

½ cup pitted mixed olives (such as Kalamata and Castelvetrano), coarsely chopped

⅓ cup chopped fresh Italian parsley

2 tablespoons fresh lemon juice

2 tablespoons olive oil

1 tablespoon red wine vinegar

Salt and pepper

1 Place the vermouth, garlic, oregano, and peppercorns in the pot. Select **SAUTÉ** and adjust to **MORE/HIGH** heat. Simmer for 1 minute to burn off some of the alcohol. Press **CANCEL**.

2 Cut the squid bodies into ½-inch-wide rings and cut the tentacle pieces in half if they are large. Add the squid and broth to the pot. Lock on the lid, select the **PRESSURE COOK** function, and adjust to **HIGH** pressure for 10 minutes. Make sure the steam valve is in the "Sealing" position and that the "Keep Warm" button is off.

3 When the cooking time is up, let the pressure come down naturally for 10 minutes and then quick-release the remaining pressure. Use a slotted spoon to transfer the squid to a large serving bowl. Strain the cooking liquid and reserve it for another use (it's lovely in seafood risotto or a fish stew). Refrigerate the squid for 10 minutes, until cooled to roughly room temperature.

4 Add the tomato, olives, parsley, lemon juice, oil, and vinegar to the squid and toss to combine. Season with salt and pepper.

The salad can be stored in an airtight container in the refrigerator for up to 24 hours.

SAVORY PARMESAN CUSTARDS WITH RED BELL PEPPER SAUCE

Serves 6   Active time: 20 minutes   Total time: 1 hour 10 minutes

Called *sformati* in Italian, these rich, savory custards are a breeze to make in the Instant Pot. They are usually served as an elegant first course, but they also make a great brunch or lunch entrée when served with a green salad. For the best flavor, grate real Parmigiano-Reggiano cheese right before folding it into the custard base; pre-grated cheese won't pack the same flavorful punch.

2   tablespoons unsalted butter

2   tablespoons all-purpose flour

2⅓ cups whole milk

3   large eggs

1½   cups freshly grated Parmesan cheese

¼   teaspoon salt, plus more as needed

⅛   teaspoon ground white pepper, plus more as needed

1   cup jarred roasted red peppers

1   tablespoon olive oil

½   teaspoon balsamic vinegar

½   small garlic clove

6   small fresh basil leaves, for garnish

1 Spray six 6-ounce oven-safe ramekins with cooking spray.

2 Place the butter in the pot, select **SAUTÉ**, and adjust to **NORMAL/ MEDIUM** heat. When the butter has melted, whisk in the flour and cook, stirring continuously, for 1 minute. Gradually whisk in the milk and cook, stirring frequently with a rubber spatula, until the mixture is thickened and bubbling, about 10 minutes. Press **CANCEL**. Scrape the milk mixture into a bowl and let cool for 5 minutes. Wash and dry the pot and return it to the appliance.

3 In a medium bowl, whisk together the eggs, cheese, salt, and white pepper. Gradually whisk in the milk mixture. Pour or ladle the custard into the prepared ramekins. Cover each ramekin tightly with foil; use plenty of foil to ensure no steam enters the ramekins.

4 Place a trivet in the pot and add 1½ cups cold water. Place the ramekins in the pot; you will need to stack them in two layers so they all fit in the appliance. Lock on the lid, select the **PRESSURE COOK** function, and adjust to **HIGH** pressure for 8 minutes. Make sure the steam valve is in the "Sealing" position and that the "Keep Warm" button is off.

5 While the custards cook, make the sauce. In a blender, combine the roasted peppers, oil, vinegar, and garlic and blend until smooth. Season with salt and white pepper and set aside.

6 When the cooking time is up, let the pressure release naturally for 10 minutes and then quick-release the remaining pressure. Test for doneness by carefully removing one ramekin from the appliance and

(recipe continues)

(*continued from page 40*)

inserting a butter knife into the center; the knife should come out clean. If the knife comes out coated with liquid custard (think melted ice cream), rewrap the ramekin with foil and return it to the pot. Lock on the lid, select **HIGH** pressure, and cook for 1 minute. Quick-release the pressure.

7 When the custards are done, blot the foil on top with paper towels to remove condensation. Remove the foil and let the custards stand at room temperature for 5 minutes.

8 Run a knife around the edges of the ramekins. Working with one ramekin at a time, place a plate on top and invert the plate and ramekin together to release the custard onto the plate.

9 Spoon the sauce around the custards and garnish with the basil. Serve warm.

The custards and sauce can be made up to 3 days in advance. Chill completely, cover with plastic, and refrigerate until ready to serve. Warm gently in the microwave before serving.

MUSHROOM AND CANNELLINI BEAN BRUSCHETTA

Serves 6 | Active time: 10 minutes | Total time: 30 minutes

The earthy flavor of mushrooms intensifies when cooked under pressure. In this recipe, meaty mushrooms cooked with cannellini beans and rosemary make a creamy, satisfying topping for grilled bread. If you can find fresh porcini mushrooms for this dish, they're worth the splurge. When porcinis are not in season, cremini mushrooms will work.

8 ounces porcini or cremini mushrooms, trimmed

2 tablespoons olive oil

1 tablespoon chopped fresh rosemary

Salt and pepper

4 medium garlic cloves, finely chopped

½ cup dry vermouth or dry white wine

2 cups Pressure-Cooked Cannellini Beans (page 197) or canned beans, drained and rinsed

1 tablespoon fresh lemon juice

12 slices Rosemary Focaccia (page 31) or small slices rustic bread

Chunk of Parmesan cheese, for garnish

1 Remove the spongy undersides of the porcini mushroom caps, if present, and discard. Cut the mushrooms lengthwise into thick bite-size wedges. Put the oil in the pot, select **SAUTÉ**, and adjust to **MORE/HIGH** heat. When the oil is hot, add the mushrooms and rosemary and season with salt and pepper. Cook, stirring occasionally, until the mushrooms give off their liquid and are starting to brown, 5 minutes. Add the garlic and cook until fragrant, 45 seconds. Add the vermouth and simmer for a minute to burn off the alcohol. Press **CANCEL**.

2 Add the beans to the pot but don't stir them into the mushrooms. Lock on the lid, select the **PRESSURE COOK** function, and adjust to **HIGH** pressure for 10 minutes. Make sure the steam valve is in the "Sealing" position and that the "Keep Warm" button is off.

3 When the cooking time is up, quick-release the pressure. Remove the lid, add the lemon juice, and stir to combine. Season with salt and pepper and set aside at room temperature.

4 Grill or toast the bread on both sides until lightly charred on the edges. Arrange the toasts on a serving platter and spoon the mushroom-bean mixture over the toasts. Using a sharp vegetable peeler, shave thin slivers of the cheese over the bruschetta.

The mushroom-bean mixture can be stored in an airtight container in the refrigerator for up to 3 days. Bring to room temperature before serving.

DEVILED EGGS WITH WHITE ANCHOVIES AND CAPERS

Serves 6 | **Active time: 10 minutes** | **Total time: 35 minutes**

Hard-boiled eggs cook perfectly under low pressure in just 12 minutes in the Instant Pot, and they're super-easy to peel. Here, they are deviled with basil, capers, and marinated white anchovies for an Italian twist. Marinated white anchovies are much milder than the salted brown variety we encounter on pizzas. Look for them in the refrigerated deli section of gourmet shops and well-stocked grocery stores or order them online. (Or omit them, if you prefer.)

6 large eggs

2 tablespoons mayonnaise

1 tablespoon chopped fresh basil

2 teaspoons finely chopped capers

2 teaspoons fresh lemon juice

Salt and pepper

6 marinated white anchovies, sliced lengthwise into 2 pieces each

1 Place 1½ cups cold water in the pot and place a steaming basket inside. Place the eggs in the steamer. Lock on the lid, select the **PRESSURE COOK** function, and adjust to **LOW** pressure for 12 minutes. Make sure the steam valve is in the "Sealing" position and that the "Keep Warm" button is off.

2 When the cooking time is up, quick-release the pressure. Transfer the eggs to a bowl of ice water and let them cool for 5 minutes. Peel the eggs and cut them in half lengthwise. Scoop the yolks into a medium bowl and mash with the mayonnaise, basil, capers, and lemon juice. Season with salt and pepper.

3 Spoon or pipe the yolk mixture back into the egg whites and top each egg with an anchovy half.

The eggs can be prepared up to 8 hours in advance and stored, loosely covered with plastic in the refrigerator until ready to serve.

QUICK GIARDINIERA

Makes 8 cups; serves 16 | Active time: 10 minutes | Total time: 25 minutes

This traditional Italian vegetable pickle normally takes at least a week of brining time. In this quick recipe, whole vegetables are briefly pressure-steamed over the aromatic pickling liquid so they become infused with flavor. Note that you set the Instant Pot to 0 minutes: The cooking will stop as soon as the Instant Pot comes up to pressure, which keeps the vegetables crisp. Serve the pickles as part of an antipasto spread, as a side dish for meats, or on Chicago-Style Italian Beef Sandwiches (page 140).

⅔ cup white vinegar

⅔ cup white wine vinegar

2 medium garlic cloves, thinly sliced

1 teaspoon salt

1 teaspoon sugar

10 whole black peppercorns

½ teaspoon fennel seeds

1 bay leaf

½ small cauliflower (about 8 ounces), left in 1 piece

1 red bell pepper, halved

½ small fennel bulb, halved lengthwise and cored

1 medium carrot, left whole

2 celery ribs, left whole

1 Place ⅔ cup cold water, the vinegars, garlic, salt, sugar, peppercorns, fennel seeds, and bay leaf in the pot. Set a steamer basket in the pot and put the vegetables in it, with the dense vegetables (cauliflower, carrot) on the bottom. Lock on the lid, select the **PRESSURE COOK** function, and adjust to **HIGH** pressure for 0 minutes. The machine will just come up to pressure and then stop. Make sure the steam valve is in the "Sealing" position and that the "Keep Warm" button is off.

2 When the cooking time is up, quick-release the remaining pressure. (It's best to do this under a ventilation hood because the steam smells strongly of vinegar.) Transfer the vegetables to a cutting board and cut them into bite-size pieces while still hot.

3 Pack the vegetables into a sterilized ½-gallon jar. Pour the hot brine from the pot over the top of the vegetables (you may not need all the liquid). Let the jar stand for at least 10 minutes before serving or let cool completely, cover, and refrigerate.

The pickles can be stored in their jar in the refrigerator for up to 1 month.

OCTOPUS, PESTO, AND POTATO SALAD

Serves 6   Active time: 10 minutes   Total time: 1 hour 10 minutes

Octopus dishes appear on menus all over Italy; my favorite are the octopus and potato salads served in Genoa, the home of basil pesto. The pressure cooker is ideal for cooking octopus: It tenderizes the meat and intensifies its flavor in just 25 minutes. The remaining cooking liquid serves as an excellent broth for seafood risotto (page 96) or seafood soup (page 52).

1   (2-pound) cleaned octopus

2   garlic cloves, peeled and left whole

2   bay leaves

    Salt

2   large waxy potatoes (about 1 pound), unpeeled

½   small red onion, thinly sliced

2   celery ribs, thinly sliced

3   tablespoons Basil Pesto (page 193) or store-bought pesto

1   tablespoon fresh lemon juice

    Pepper

1 Cut the tentacles apart into separate arms. Cut the head into large bite-size pieces. Place the octopus pieces, 2 cups cold water, the garlic, bay leaves, and 1 teaspoon salt in the pot. Set a trivet or steamer basket over the octopus and place the potatoes on top.

2 Lock on the lid, select the **PRESSURE COOK** function, and adjust to **HIGH** pressure for 25 minutes. Make sure the steam valve is in the "Sealing" position and that the "Keep Warm" button is off. Meanwhile, place the onion and celery in small bowl of ice water.

3 When the cooking time is up, quick-release the pressure. Test the potatoes and octopus; a paring knife should easily pierce them with little resistance. If you have any doubt about the octopus, cut a small piece off the thick end of a tentacle and taste it; it should be tender, not rubbery. If the ingredients are not done, lock on the lid, return the appliance to **HIGH** pressure for an additional minute or two, then quick-release the pressure. Discard the garlic and bay leaves and reserve the cooking liquid for another use.

4 When cool enough to handle, pull the peels off the potatoes and discard. Cut the potatoes into bite-size pieces and place them in a large serving bowl. Rinse off the dark, gelatinous membrane from the octopus, if desired. (Most Italian chefs leave it on, but the texture is not for everyone.) Cut the octopus into bite-size pieces and add to the bowl with the potatoes. Drain the onion and celery and add them to the bowl. Add the pesto and lemon juice and toss the salad gently to combine. Season with salt and pepper. Serve.

SOUPS AND STEWS

Soups and the Instant Pot are a match made in heaven—cooking under pressure intensifies the flavors of vegetables, cooks grains and beans quickly, and makes meats tender in minutes. With a few exceptions, you need to let the pressure come down naturally for at least 10 minutes after the cooking time is up to prevent the contents from overcooking or scorching on the bottom of the pot.

I recommend using homemade broths (see pages 198 to 201), even if you normally don't bother. Homemade broth makes a big flavor difference, and they're a breeze to make in the Instant Pot; plus, they're much healthier than store-bought broth. That said, if you don't have a stash of homemade broth, store-bought will work just fine, but choose good-quality, low-sodium options for the best results.

In many of the following recipes, you'll see that I call for Parmesan cheese rinds. It might seem like an odd ingredient, but Italian cooks know that the hard rind left over from grating Parmigiano-Reggiano cheese can infuse soups and sauces with tons of flavor. The rind is too hard to melt much, so it's discarded at the end of cooking, much like a bay leaf. If you don't happen to have a Parmigiano-Reggiano cheese rind, try asking at your local cheese shop or grocery store cheese counter: The rinds are often sold at a deep discount as a by-product of making grated cheese.

🫕 LIGURIAN FISH SOUP

Serves 4   Active time: 25 minutes   Total time: 1 hour

There's a different version of this delicious fish and fennel soup, called *buridda*,
in every harbor of northwestern Italy. Local red mullet or bass is traditional,
but I opt for extra-firm fish like sustainable swordfish, halibut, or thick
cod fillets, as they hold their shape better in the Instant Pot.

1   tablespoon olive oil

1   medium yellow onion, chopped

1   medium fennel bulb, cored and chopped

1   small red bell pepper, chopped

2   tablespoons chopped fresh oregano, or 1½ teaspoons dried

4   medium garlic cloves, finely chopped

1   tablespoon tomato paste

½   cup dry vermouth or dry white wine

3   cups Homemade Seafood Broth (page 200) or store-bought seafood broth, or 2 cups bottled clam juice plus 1 cup water

2   medium (8-ounce) waxy potatoes, peeled and cut into ½-inch chunks

¾   cup boxed or canned diced tomatoes in puree

1   bay leaf
    Salt and pepper

1   pound firm white fish steaks, 1 to 1½ inches thick

12   ounces clams and/or mussels, rinsed, debearded if using mussels
    Crusty bread, sliced and toasted, for serving

1   lemon, cut into wedges, for serving

1 Put the oil in the pot, select **SAUTÉ**, and adjust to **NORMAL/MEDIUM** heat. When the oil is hot, add the onion, fennel, bell pepper, and oregano and cook, stirring occasionally, until tender, 5 minutes. Add the garlic and tomato paste and cook, stirring frequently, until the garlic is fragrant, 45 seconds. Add the vermouth and simmer to burn off some of the alcohol, 1 minute. Press **CANCEL**.

2 Add the broth, potatoes, tomatoes, bay leaf, ½ teaspoon salt, and several grinds of black pepper. Place the fish on top of the top of the vegetables, but do not submerge it. Lock on the lid, select the **PRESSURE COOK** function, and adjust to **HIGH** pressure for 5 minutes. Make sure the steam valve is in the "Sealing" position and that the "Keep Warm" button is off.

3 When the cooking time is up, quick-release the pressure. Use a slotted spoon to transfer the fish to a cutting board. If using swordfish, remove the skin, if present, and discard. Cut the fish into bite-size pieces and set aside.

4 Add the clams and/or mussels to the pot and stir very gently to submerge them in the cooking liquid. Select **SAUTÉ**, adjust to **LESS/LOW** heat, and cook, uncovered, until the shells open, 5 to 8 minutes. Discard any unopened shellfish. Season the soup with salt and black pepper and discard the bay leaf. Return the fish to the pot and stir gently to combine. Press **CANCEL**.

5 Serve the stew with the bread and lemon wedges on the side.

 MINESTRONE

Serves 4   Active time: 15 minutes   Total time: 35 minutes

Comforting and packed with veggies, this perennial favorite is ready in just 35 minutes, but tastes like it has been bubbling away on the stove for hours. The vegetables you use are adaptable; just keep in mind that firm vegetables (squash, potatoes, etc.) should be added during the first phase of cooking under pressure and more tender ingredients (peas, leafy greens) added at the end and simmered on the "Sauté" function so they retain their texture.

2	tablespoons olive oil
1	medium yellow onion, chopped
1	large carrot, chopped
2	celery ribs, chopped
2	medium garlic cloves, finely chopped
½	cup dry vermouth or dry white wine
4	cups Homemade Vegetable, Chicken, or Beef Broth (pages 198 to 201) or low-sodium store-bought broth
1¼	cups canned crushed tomatoes
1½	cups large cauliflower florets (2-inch pieces)
1	(2-inch) Parmesan cheese rind (optional)
1½	cups Pressure-Cooked Borlotti or Cannellini Beans (page 197), or 1 (14-ounce) can beans, drained and rinsed
1	medium (8-ounce) zucchini, chopped
1	cup green beans, trimmed and cut into bite-size pieces
1	(2-inch) sprig rosemary
	Salt and pepper
¼	cup finely chopped fresh basil leaves

1 Put the oil in the pot, select **SAUTÉ**, and adjust to **NORMAL/MEDIUM** heat. When the oil is hot, add the onion, carrot, and celery and cook, stirring occasionally, until tender, 4 minutes. Add the garlic and cook until fragrant, 45 seconds.

2 Add the vermouth and cook for 1 minute to burn off some of the alcohol. Press **CANCEL**. Add the broth, tomatoes, cauliflower, and cheese rind (if using). Lock on the lid, select the **PRESSURE COOK** function, and adjust to **HIGH** pressure for 5 minutes. Make sure the steam valve is in the "Sealing" position and that the "Keep Warm" button is off.

3 When the cooking time is up, quick-release the pressure. Add the borlotti beans, zucchini, green beans, and rosemary sprig. Select **SAUTÉ** and adjust to **LESS/LOW** heat. Simmer, uncovered, stirring occasionally, until the zucchini is just tender, 10 minutes. Press **CANCEL**. Discard the cheese rind and rosemary sprig. Season the soup with salt and pepper.

4 Ladle the soup into bowls and garnish with the basil.

The soup can be stored in an airtight container in the refrigerator for up to 5 days. Reheat gently before serving.

ONE POT ITALIAN WEDDING SOUP

Serves 4 | Active time: 10 minutes | Total time: 50 minutes

This lovely, light soup is called *minestra maritata*, or "married soup,"
in Italian because the meatballs in it marry so well with the flavor of escarole.
Escarole looks like a big, leafy head of romaine, but it is sturdier and has a
likeable touch of bitterness that Italians seek out. You can substitute another
green—dandelion, baby mustard greens, or Swiss chard work well.

1 pound ground turkey (a mix of dark and white meat)

¼ cup dry Italian-style bread crumbs

3 tablespoons grated Parmesan cheese

1 egg yolk

1 tablespoon finely chopped fresh Italian parsley

1 teaspoon finely grated lemon zest

¾ teaspoon salt

½ teaspoon granulated garlic

¼ teaspoon freshly grated nutmeg

Pepper

7 cups Homemade Chicken Broth (page 198) or low-sodium store-bought broth

⅓ cup fregola (toasted pearl-shaped pasta), pearl couscous, or orzo

1 (2-inch) Parmesan cheese rind (optional)

4 cups escarole leaves, torn into bite-size pieces

1 tablespoon fresh lemon juice

1 In a medium bowl, mix the turkey, bread crumbs, cheese, egg yolk, parsley, lemon zest, salt, granulated garlic, nutmeg, and a few grinds of pepper until thoroughly blended. Form the mixture into 16 meatballs, about 1 heaping tablespoon each.

2 Place the meatballs, broth, fregola, and cheese rind (if using) in the pot. Lock on the lid, select the **PRESSURE COOK** function, and adjust to **HIGH** pressure for 5 minutes. Make sure the steam valve is in the "Sealing" position and that the "Keep Warm" button is off.

3 When the cooking time is up, let the pressure come down naturally for 10 minutes and then quick-release the remaining pressure. Remove the lid and add the escarole to the pot. Select **SAUTÉ**, adjust to **LESS/LOW** heat, and cook until the greens are wilted and tender, 2 minutes. Press **CANCEL**. Discard the cheese rind and add the lemon juice to the soup. Season with salt and pepper.

TORTELLINI SOUP WITH SPRING VEGETABLES

Serves 4   Active time: 10 minutes   Total time: 45 minutes

This soup, a staple in the Emilia-Romagna region, is so simple that you really must use homemade chicken broth to make it work . . . good thing making broth in the Instant Pot is so easy and rewarding! Use dried cheese tortellini for this soup; fresh tortellini will fall apart and overcook under pressure. The parsley–lemon zest garnish, called *gremolata* in Italian, adds a bright, lemony punch.

6	cups Homemade Chicken Broth (page 198) or low-sodium store-bought broth
1	(9-ounce) package dried tortellini
1	cup fresh or frozen green peas
1	small carrot, thinly sliced into coins
1	(3-inch) Parmesan cheese rind (optional)
2	tablespoons fresh Italian parsley leaves
1½	teaspoons finely grated lemon zest
½	small garlic clove
	Salt and pepper

1 Combine the broth, tortellini, peas, carrot, and cheese rind (if using) in the pot. Lock on the lid, select the **PRESSURE COOK** function, and adjust to **HIGH** pressure for 10 minutes. Make sure the steam valve is in the "Sealing" position and that the "Keep Warm" button is off.

2 While the soup is cooking, make the gremolata: Mound the parsley, lemon zest, and garlic on a cutting board. Sprinkle with a few pinches of salt and chop everything together until you've got a slightly moist, finely chopped mixture.

3 When the soup cooking time is up, let the pressure come down naturally for 10 minutes, then quick-release the remaining pressure. Season the soup with salt and pepper and discard the cheese rind.

4 Ladle the soup into bowls and sprinkle with the gremolata.

PORCINI DUMPLINGS IN BROTH

Serves 4   Active time: 10 minutes   Total time: 45 minutes

These light bread dumplings bobbing in rich chicken broth are a staple in the mountainous Alto Adige region of northeastern Italy. This dish is so simple that you really do want to use a more flavorful homemade broth. The dumplings by themselves can be poached in salted water and served as a side dish for roasts.

¼ cup dried porcini mushrooms (¼ ounce)

½ cup milk

1 large egg

2 tablespoons finely chopped fresh basil or Italian parsley

5 ounces stale hearty white bread, cut into ¼-inch cubes (2¾ cups)

1 medium shallot, finely chopped

¼ cup plus 3 tablespoons grated Parmesan cheese

Salt and pepper

¼ teaspoon freshly grated nutmeg

⅔ cup all-purpose flour

5½ cups Homemade Chicken Broth (page 198) or low-sodium store-bought broth

1. In a microwave-safe measuring cup, combine the dried mushrooms with ½ cup water and microwave on high heat for 1 minute to soften. (Alternatively, soak the mushrooms in the same amount of boiling water for 30 minutes.) Finely chop the mushrooms and reserve the soaking liquid.

2. In a large bowl, whisk together the milk, egg, and basil. Add the bread cubes, shallot, 3 tablespoons of the cheese, ½ teaspoon salt, a few grinds of pepper, and the nutmeg and stir to combine. Sprinkle the flour over the bread mixture and stir until the mixture forms a sticky dough. Let stand for 10 minutes at room temperature to make the mixture easier to handle.

3. Add the mushroom soaking liquid to the pot, except for the last gritty tablespoon or so of the liquid (discard that bit). Add the broth, select **SAUTÉ**, and adjust to **MORE/HIGH** heat. While the broth is heating up, form the dough with moist hands into 12 golf ball–size dumplings. Add them to the broth. Press **CANCEL**.

4. Lock on the lid, select the **PRESSURE COOK** function, and adjust to **HIGH** pressure for 5 minutes. Make sure the steam valve is in the "Sealing" position and that the "Keep Warm" button is off.

5. When the cooking time is up, let the pressure come down naturally for 10 minutes and then quick-release the remaining pressure.

6. Ladle the soup and dumplings into bowls. Sprinkle with the remaining ¼ cup cheese.

UMBRIAN LENTIL AND CROUTON SOUP

Serves 4   Active time: 20 minutes   Total time: 1 hour

Castelluccio, a tiny town in Umbria, is famous for its brown lentils, and for good reason. The small, brown lentils become creamy and tender when simmered, but retain their shape without falling apart. They can be found at gourmet shops or ordered online. Or use small, dark green French *lentilles du Puy* or Spanish *pardina* lentils if you can't find the Castelluccio variety.

2   tablespoons olive oil

1   medium yellow onion, chopped

1   medium carrot, chopped

2   celery ribs, chopped

1   medium parsnip, peeled and chopped

2   teaspoons chopped fresh thyme, or ½ teaspoon dried

6   medium garlic cloves, finely chopped

1   tablespoon tomato paste

4   cups Homemade Chicken or Vegetable Broth (page 198 or 201) or low-sodium store-bought broth

1   cup Castelluccio brown lentils

¼   cup Arborio rice

2   bay leaves

2   cups bite-size cubes Rosemary Focaccia (page 31) or store-bought focaccia

Salt and pepper

1 Preheat the oven to 350°F.

2 Put the oil in the pot, select **SAUTÉ**, and adjust to **NORMAL/MEDIUM** heat. When the oil is hot, add the onion, carrot, celery, parsnip, and thyme and cook, stirring frequently, until the vegetables are tender, 4 minutes. Add the garlic and tomato paste and cook until fragrant, 45 seconds. Press **CANCEL**.

3 Add the broth, lentils, rice, and bay leaves. Lock on the lid, select the **PRESSURE COOK** function, and adjust to **HIGH** pressure for 15 minutes. Make sure the steam valve is in the "Sealing" position and that the "Keep Warm" button is off.

4 While the soup is cooking, make the croutons: Arrange the focaccia cubes in an even layer on a small baking sheet and bake, stirring occasionally, until crispy, 10 minutes. Set aside.

5 When the cooking time is up, let the pressure come down naturally for 10 minutes and then quick-release the remaining pressure. Season the soup with salt and pepper.

6 Ladle the soup into bowls and garnish each with a handful of the croutons.

The soup, without croutons, can be stored in an airtight container in the refrigerator for up to 5 days. Reheat gently before serving.

BEAN AND SPECK SOUP

Serves 4 | Active time: 15 minutes | Total time: 50 minutes

Speck is a lightly smoked and cured ham similar to prosciutto from the Alto Adige region. It's served as a cold antipasto with bread and red wine in Northern Italy, but it's also used to add delicious smoky, woodsy flavor to dishes like this simple bean soup. You can find speck where Italian products like prosciutto are sold; ask for a thick slice so you can dice the meat for added texture in the soup. If you're unable to find speck, a thick slice of prosciutto will do in a pinch.

2	tablespoons olive oil
1	medium yellow onion, chopped
1	medium carrot, chopped
1	celery rib, chopped
¾	cup chopped speck (4 ounces)
6	medium garlic cloves, chopped
3	cups Homemade Chicken or Vegetable Broth (page 198 or 201) or low-sodium store-bought broth
3	cups soaked cannellini or borlotti beans (from 1½ cups dry beans; see page 196)
2	bay leaves
	Salt and pepper
	Pinch of red chile flakes (optional)
1	(3-inch) sprig fresh rosemary

1 Put the oil in the pot, select **SAUTÉ**, and adjust to **NORMAL/MEDIUM** heat. When the oil is hot, add the onion, carrot, celery, and speck and cook, stirring frequently, until the vegetables are tender and the fat in the speck has rendered, 8 minutes. Add the garlic and cook until fragrant, 45 seconds. Press **CANCEL**.

2 Add the broth, beans, bay leaves, ½ teaspoon salt, a few grinds of pepper, and the red chile flakes. Lock on the lid, select the **PRESSURE COOK** function, and adjust to **HIGH** pressure for 20 minutes. Make sure the steam valve is in the "Sealing" position and that the "Keep Warm" button is off.

3 When the cooking time is up, let the pressure come down naturally for 10 minutes and then quick-release the remaining pressure. Unlock the lid and plunge the rosemary into the pot. Select **SAUTÉ**, adjust to **NORMAL/MEDIUM** heat, and simmer, uncovered, stirring occasionally, for 5 minutes. Press **CANCEL**. Discard the rosemary sprig and bay leaves. Season with salt and pepper.

The soup can be stored in an airtight container in the refrigerator for up to 5 days or in the freezer for up to 3 months. Reheat gently before serving.

ONE

BUTTERNUT SQUASH, BARLEY, AND CHESTNUT SOUP

ONE POT

Serves 6 | Active time: 20 minutes | Total time: 1 hour 20 minutes

Italians love chestnuts—they make flour out of them for cakes, put them in soups, use them in stuffing, and eat fire-roasted chestnuts as a street snack in late autumn. Peeling and roasting chestnuts is time-consuming, so I use the pre-roasted peeled sort that come in glass jars or Cryovac packages; look for them at specialty markets and online. A sprinkle of Piave Vecchio, a smooth, nutty cow's-milk cheese from the Veneto, echoes the nutty sweetness of the chestnuts.

2 tablespoons olive oil

1 medium yellow onion, chopped

1 medium carrot, chopped

1 celery rib, chopped

2 teaspoons minced fresh sage, or 1 teaspoon dried

2 medium garlic cloves, finely chopped

6 cups Homemade Chicken or Vegetable Broth (page 198 or 201) or low-sodium store-bought broth

1 medium (1½-pound) butternut squash, peeled, seeded, and chopped (about 3 cups)

1 (8-ounce) jar peeled roasted chestnuts, chopped

½ cup whole-grain barley or semi-pearled barley (do not use pearled barley)

½ teaspoon ground ginger

1 bay leaf

Salt and pepper

½ cup finely grated Piave Vecchio or Parmesan cheese

1 Put the oil in the pot, select **SAUTÉ**, and adjust to **NORMAL/MEDIUM** heat. When the oil is hot, add the onion, carrot, celery, and sage and cook, stirring frequently, until the vegetables begin to brown, 8 minutes. Add the garlic and cook until fragrant, 45 seconds. Press **CANCEL**.

2 Add the broth, squash, chestnuts, barley, ginger, and bay leaf to the pot. Lock on the lid, select the **PRESSURE COOK** function, and adjust to **HIGH** pressure for 30 minutes. Make sure the steam valve is in the "Sealing" position and that the "Keep Warm" button is off.

3 When the cooking time is up, let the pressure come down naturally for 15 minutes and then quick-release the remaining pressure. Discard the bay leaf. Mash about half the squash pieces against the side of the pot with a wooden spoon to thicken the soup slightly. Season the soup with salt and pepper.

 Serve with the cheese sprinkled on top.

The soup can be stored in an airtight container in the refrigerator for up to 5 days. Reheat gently before serving.

CANNELLINI, KALE, AND BREAD SOUP

ONE POT

| Serves 6 | Active time: 20 minutes | Total time: 1 hour 25 minutes |

This thick Tuscan soup is called *ribollita*, Italian for "re-boiled," because it's traditionally made with leftover beans, vegetables, and stale bread. But this version starts fresh with quick-soaked cannellini beans, delicate savoy cabbage, and sturdy lacinato kale, ribs and all—the Instant Pot makes them all meltingly tender in no time.

2 tablespoons olive oil, plus more for garnish

¼ cup diced pancetta, from a ½-inch-thick slab, or chopped thick-cut bacon

1 medium yellow onion, chopped

1 carrot, finely diced

1 celery rib, finely diced

3 garlic cloves, chopped

4 cups chopped savoy cabbage

4 cups chopped lacinato kale, including center ribs

4 cups Homemade Chicken or Vegetable Broth (page 198 or 201) or low-sodium store-bought broth

3 cups soaked cannellini beans (from 1½ cups dried beans; see page 196)

1 (2-inch) Parmesan cheese rind (optional)

Pinch of red chile flakes

Salt and pepper

2 cups 1-inch pieces rustic bread (4 ounces), crusts discarded

½ cup Homemade Marinara (page 192) or jarred sauce, warmed

1 Put the oil in the pot, select **SAUTÉ**, and adjust to **MORE/HIGH** heat. When the oil is hot, add the pancetta and cook, stirring occasionally, until it begins to brown, 2 minutes. Carefully spoon out all but 1 tablespoon of the fat. Add the onion, carrot, and celery to the pot and cook, stirring, until the onion is just tender, 4 minutes. Add the garlic and cook until fragrant, 45 seconds. Press **CANCEL**.

2 Add the cabbage, kale, broth, beans, cheese rind (if using), red chile flakes, ½ teaspoon salt, and several grinds of pepper. Lock on the lid, select the **PRESSURE COOK** function, and adjust to **HIGH** pressure for 15 minutes. Make sure the steam valve is in the "Sealing" position and that the "Keep Warm" button is off.

3 When the cooking time is up, let the pressure come down naturally for 10 minutes and then quick-release the remaining pressure. Stir the bread and marinara sauce into the soup and let stand for 2 minutes. Discard the cheese rind and season the soup with salt and pepper.

4 Ladle the soup into bowls and garnish with a drizzle of olive oil, if desired.

The soup can be stored in an airtight container in the refrigerator for up to 5 days. Reheat gently before serving.

CREAMY MUSHROOM SOUP WITH TRUFFLE CHEESE TOASTS

Serves 4 Active time: 20 minutes Total time: 40 minutes

Porcini means "little pigs" in Italian, an apt name for the squat, plump wild mushrooms that are prized by cooks in Italy. They grow wild in the U.S., too, but are unfortunately rather rare. This recipe uses easier-to-find dried porcini and flavorful shiitake mushrooms. They're paired with little dippable toasts cloaked in melted truffle-infused cheese.

1 ounce dried porcini mushrooms (about 1 cup)

2 tablespoons unsalted butter

2 large leeks, white and light green parts only, thinly sliced crosswise and rinsed well

8 ounces shiitake mushrooms, stemmed and sliced

2 teaspoons chopped fresh thyme, or ½ teaspoon dried

Salt and pepper

¼ cup dry sherry or dry white wine

3 cups Homemade Chicken or Vegetable Broth (page 198 or 201) or low-sodium store-bought broth

1 medium (8-ounce) russet potato, peeled and chopped

8 slices Rosemary Focaccia (page 31) or baguette

½ cup grated truffle cheese, such as pecorino tartufo

½ cup heavy cream (optional)

1 In a microwave-safe measuring cup, combine 2 cups water and the dried mushrooms and microwave on high heat for 1 minute to soften. (Alternatively, soak the mushrooms in the same amount of boiling water for 30 minutes.) Set aside.

2 Place the butter in the pot, select **SAUTÉ**, and adjust to **MORE/HIGH** heat. When the butter has melted, add the leeks, shiitake mushrooms, thyme, and a few pinches of salt and cook, stirring frequently, until the vegetables are tender, 4 minutes. Add the sherry and cook for 1 minute, scraping up any browned bits at the bottom of the pot.

3 Transfer the porcini mushrooms and most of the soaking liquid to the pot, discarding the last tablespoon or so of gritty liquid at the bottom of the measuring cup. Add the broth and potatoes. Lock on the lid, select the **PRESSURE COOK** function, and adjust to **HIGH** pressure for 8 minutes. Make sure the steam valve is in the "Sealing" position and that the "Keep Warm" button is off.

4 While the soup is cooking, make the truffle toasts: Preheat the broiler and adjust the oven rack so it is 6 inches below the broiler element. Cut the focaccia into ¼-inch-thick slices about 3 inches long. Place the bread on a baking sheet and sprinkle with the cheese. Broil until the cheese is bubbling, 3 minutes.

(recipe continues)

(continued from page 66)

 When the cooking time is up, let the pressure come down naturally for 10 minutes and then quick-release the remaining pressure. Add the cream (if using) and blend the soup with an immersion blender until smooth. (Alternatively, working in batches, carefully transfer the soup to a blender and blend with the lid slightly ajar to allow steam to escape.) Season the soup with salt and pepper.

Serve the soup with cheese toasts on the side.

The soup can be stored in an airtight container in the refrigerator for up to 5 days. Reheat gently before serving.

CREAMY ZUCCHINI SOUP

Serves 4 | Active time: 10 minutes | Total time: 50 minutes

There's a wide array of *vellutata*, or "cream of," vegetable soups in Italy. This particular recipe is the perfect solution for a bumper crop of zucchini. The high pressure in the Instant Pot intensifies the flavors and makes for an incredibly silky soup; even my zucchini-hating husband likes it! The recipe is quite adaptable—try it with the same weight of broccoli, cauliflower, or butternut squash, but increase the broth to 1¾ cups.

1 tablespoon unsalted butter

1 large shallot, chopped

1½ pounds zucchini, coarsely chopped

1 cup Homemade Chicken or Vegetable Broth (page 198 or 201) or low-sodium store-bought broth

1 large (12-ounce) russet potato, peeled and chopped

   Salt and pepper

½ cup heavy cream

½ teaspoon freshly grated nutmeg

1 tablespoon finely chopped fresh chives

1 Put the butter in the pot, select **SAUTÉ**, and adjust to **NORMAL/MEDIUM** heat. When the butter has melted, add the shallot and cook, stirring frequently, until it begins to brown, 4 minutes. Press **CANCEL**.

2 Add the zucchini, broth, potato, ½ teaspoon salt, and a few grinds of pepper and stir to combine. Lock on the lid, select the **PRESSURE COOK** function, and adjust to **HIGH** pressure for 15 minutes. Make sure the steam valve is in the "Sealing" position and that the "Keep Warm" button is off.

3 When the cooking time is up, let the pressure come down naturally for 10 minutes and then quick-release the remaining pressure. Add the cream and nutmeg and puree the soup with an immersion blender. (Alternatively, working in batches, carefully transfer the soup to a blender and blend with the lid slightly ajar to allow steam to escape.) Season the soup with salt and pepper.

4 Serve garnished with the chives.

The soup can be stored in an airtight container in the refrigerator for up to 5 days. Reheat gently before serving.

TUSCAN BEEF AND PEPPER STEW

Serves 4 to 6 · Active time: 15 minutes · Total time: 1 hour

There's a different version of *peposo* in every home in Tuscany, including ultra-minimalist recipes that call for just three ingredients: beef, a whole bottle of Chianti, and a big handful of black peppercorns! In this version, there are also some vegetables and just enough coarsely ground pepper to add a little belly-warming heat. Serve the stew with a warm loaf of country bread for scooping up the delicious broth.

2 pounds chuck roast, fat trimmed, cut into 2-inch pieces

2 tablespoons olive oil

1½ teaspoons salt

2 teaspoons coarsely ground black pepper

½ cup Chianti or other dry red wine

1 cup canned crushed tomatoes

1 medium yellow onion, chopped

2 large carrots, coarsely chopped

8 ounces cremini mushrooms, quartered

¾ cup Homemade Beef Broth (page 199) or low-sodium store-bought broth

¼ cup oil-packed sun-dried tomatoes, drained and chopped

3 medium garlic cloves, finely chopped

3 whole cloves

¼ cup finely chopped fresh Italian parsley

1 Preheat the broiler and adjust the oven rack so that it is 6 inches below the broiling element. Line a rimmed baking sheet with foil.

2 Toss the beef with 1 tablespoon of the oil and the salt and pepper on the prepared baking sheet. Arrange the meat in a single layer on the baking sheet and broil, stirring once, until the meat is well browned, 12 minutes. (Alternatively, brown the meat in the pot: Add the oil to the pot, select **SAUTÉ**, adjust to **MORE/HIGH** heat, and brown the meat in small batches in the hot oil.)

3 Place the meat and any accumulated juices from the baking sheet in the pot. Select **SAUTÉ** and adjust to **MORE/HIGH** heat, then add the wine and simmer until reduced slightly, 5 minutes. Add the remaining ingredients and lock on the lid. Select the **PRESSURE COOK** function and adjust to **HIGH** pressure for 25 minutes. Make sure the steam valve is in the "Sealing" position and that the "Keep Warm" button is off.

4 When the cooking time is up, let the pressure come down naturally for 10 minutes and then quick-release the remaining pressure. Season the stew with salt and pepper.

The stew can be stored in an airtight container in the refrigerator for up to 5 days or in the freezer for up to 3 months. Reheat gently before serving.

PASTA AND GRAINS

The Instant Pot is an obvious choice for making pasta sauces—the high pressure mingles and quickly melds tomatoes, aromatics, meat, and vegetables into brilliant sauces that taste like they've been simmering on the stove for hours.

While doing research for the pasta sauces in this book, I came across a neat trick from the good folks at *Cooks Illustrated* for making meat sauces taste meatier—the addition of a small amount of baking soda. The alkaline nature of baking soda encourages the Maillard reaction, which gives you sweet, caramelized flavor and "beefs up" sauces like the ones here. Because the sauces are rather thick, you may encounter a bit of browned tomato at the bottom of the pot—these bits are deliciously caramelized! Stir any browned bits at the bottom of the pot into the rest of the sauce; they're a big flavor booster.

The Instant Pot is great at tackling more than just pasta sauces. You can also cook pasta *and* the sauce all at once. There are nine recipes in this chapter that use this trick, from light penne with tuna and cherry tomato sauce to rich and creamy spaghetti carbonara. The finished pastas may initially look too saucy, but after a few minutes standing time, the pasta absorbs the cooking liquid to arrive at a dish that's just right. For strand pasta, you may encounter a few clumps—just stir after cooking to remove the kinks. You can even make lasagna with the "pot within a pot" method—the ingredients go into a springform pan, the pan is set on a trivet above some water in the pot, and the whole thing is cooked under pressure in minutes!

My family loves risotto, but all the stirring required to achieve creamy risotto gives me pause. In this chapter, you'll find four recipes for comforting risottos that are done in minutes, no stirring required. Polenta, too, is cooked to creamy perfection with just the press of a button.

SHORT RIB RAGÙ

Serves 8 | Active time: 20 minutes | Total time: 1 hour 40 minutes

This sauce tastes even better the day after it is made and freezes well, so this recipe makes a big batch with the intention that you will freeze half for later. Serve the sauce tossed with wide, flat pasta such as pappardelle or spoon it over creamy polenta (see pages 97 and 102).

2 pounds meaty beef short ribs

2 tablespoons olive oil

Salt and pepper

1 onion, finely chopped

1 large carrot, finely chopped

1 celery rib, finely chopped

1½ teaspoons dried Italian seasoning

½ teaspoon baking soda

3 medium garlic cloves, chopped

3 tablespoons tomato paste

½ cup dry red wine, such as Chianti or Nebbiolo

1 (28-ounce) can crushed tomatoes

½ cup Homemade Beef Broth (page 199) or low-sodium store-bought broth

2 tablespoons dried porcini mushrooms (optional), rinsed to remove grit

1 (4-inch) Parmesan cheese rind (optional)

1. Select **SAUTÉ** and adjust to **MORE/HIGH** heat. Brush the short ribs with 1 tablespoon of the oil and season liberally with salt and pepper. When the oil is hot, add the short ribs to the pot, meaty side down, and cook until well browned, 8 minutes. (You may need to brown the ribs in batches.) Transfer the short ribs to a plate.

2. Put the remaining 1 tablespoon oil in the pot. Add the onion, carrot, celery, Italian seasoning, and baking soda and cook, stirring, until the onion is tender, 4 minutes. Stir in the garlic and tomato paste and cook for 1 minute. Add the wine and cook for 1 minute to burn off some of the alcohol. Press **CANCEL**.

3. Add the short ribs and any accumulated juices on the plate, the tomatoes, broth, dried mushrooms (if using), and cheese rind (if using) and stir gently to combine. Lock on the lid, select the **PRESSURE COOK** function, and adjust to **HIGH** pressure for 40 minutes. Make sure the steam valve is in "Sealing" position and that the "Keep Warm" button is off.

4. When the cooking time is up, let the pressure come down naturally for 10 minutes and then quick-release the remaining pressure. Transfer the short ribs to a cutting board and shred the meat; discard the fat and bones.

5. Select **SAUTÉ** and adjust to **NORMAL/MEDIUM** heat. When the liquid comes to a simmer, liquid fat will pool on the top around the edges of the pot. Spoon this off and discard it. Discard the cheese rind. Return the meat to the sauce and season with salt and pepper. Press **CANCEL**.

The sauce can be stored in an airtight container in the refrigerator for up to 5 days or in the freezer for up to 3 months. Reheat gently before serving.

BOLOGNESE SAUCE

Makes 6 cups; serves 8   Active time: 20 minutes   Total time: 1 hour, 15 minutes

The high pressure of the Instant Pot extracts every bit of flavor from the ingredients in this recipe to deliver a rich, meaty sauce that tastes like your Italian grandma made it. Serve the sauce old-school style over spaghetti or try it on potato gnocchi.

8   ounces ground beef (preferably ground chuck)

8   ounces ground pork

2   tablespoons olive oil

1   medium yellow onion, finely chopped

1   large carrot, finely chopped

1   celery rib, finely chopped

¼   cup diced pancetta, from a ½-inch-thick slab, or chopped thick-cut bacon

¼   teaspoon baking soda

¼   cup tomato paste

½   cup dry vermouth or dry white wine

2   cups canned crushed tomatoes

½   cup Homemade Beef Broth (page 199) or low-sodium store-bought broth

1   (3-inch) Parmesan cheese rind (optional)

1   bay leaf

½   cup heavy cream (optional)

Salt and pepper

1 Select **SAUTÉ** and adjust to **MORE/HIGH** heat. When the pot is hot, add the ground beef and pork and cook, stirring occasionally, until no longer pink, 8 minutes. Transfer to a colander to drain off the fat.

2 Return the pot to the appliance and add the oil. Add the onion, carrot, celery, pancetta, and baking soda and cook, stirring occasionally, until the vegetables are tender, 5 minutes. Add the tomato paste and cook, stirring continuously, until it begins to brown, 1 minute. Add the vermouth and simmer for 1 minute to burn off some of the alcohol, scraping up any browned bits on the bottom of the pot. Press **CANCEL**.

3 Return the meat to the pot and add the tomatoes, broth, cheese rind (if using), and bay leaf. Lock on the lid, select the **PRESSURE COOK** function, and adjust to **HIGH** pressure for 30 minutes. Make sure the steam valve is in the "Sealing" position and that the "Keep Warm" button is off.

4 When the cooking time is up, let the pressure come down naturally for 10 minutes, then quick-release the remaining pressure. Discard the cheese rind and bay leaf. Add the cream (if using), and stir to combine. Taste the sauce and season with salt and pepper.

The sauce can be stored in an airtight container in the refrigerator for up to 5 days or in the freezer for up to 3 months. Reheat gently before serving.

LAMB RAGÙ

This Southern Italian pasta sauce is made with bone-in lamb steaks braised with tomatoes, fennel, pancetta, and marjoram. The bones and connective tissue from cheaper cuts like arm or blade chops add meaty flavor and body to the sauce and are much thriftier than pricy leg of lamb. Toss the ragù with rigatoni or *mafalde*, long strips of pasta with frilled edges. Finish the dish with fresh mint and fresh mozzarella to offset the richness of the meat.

3   **bone-in lamb arm or blade steaks (1¾ to 2 pounds total)**

2   **tablespoons olive oil**

    Salt and pepper

1   **medium yellow onion, chopped**

1   **medium carrot, chopped**

¼   **cup chopped fennel stalks or bulb**

¼   **cup diced pancetta, from a ½-inch-thick slab, or chopped thick-cut bacon**

1   **teaspoon dried marjoram or oregano**

½   **teaspoon baking soda**

3   **medium garlic cloves, finely chopped**

2   **tablespoons tomato paste**

½   **cup dry southern Italian red wine, such as Primitivo**

1   **(28-ounce) can whole peeled San Marzano tomatoes, chopped (see Note, page 192), with their juices**

¼   **to ½ teaspoon red chile flakes**

1   **(8-ounce) ball fresh mozzarella cheese, torn into shreds or sliced**

¼   **cup torn fresh mint leaves**

1   Select **SAUTÉ** and adjust to **MORE/HIGH** heat. When the pot is hot, brush the lamb steaks with 1 tablespoon of the oil and season liberally with salt and black pepper. Working in two batches, sear the steaks until browned, 3 to 4 minutes per side. Transfer to a plate.

2   Add the remaining 1 tablespoon oil to the pot. Add the onion, carrot, fennel, pancetta, marjoram, and baking soda and cook until tender, 5 minutes. Add the garlic and tomato paste and cook until fragrant, 45 seconds. Add the wine and simmer for 1 minute to boil off some of the alcohol. Press **CANCEL**.

3   Return the lamb and any accumulated juices on the plate to the pot. Add the tomatoes and red chile flakes and stir to combine. Lock on the lid, select the **PRESSURE COOK** function, and adjust to **HIGH** pressure for 30 minutes. Make sure the steam valve is in the "Sealing" position and that the "Keep Warm" button is off.

4   When cooking time is up, let the pressure come down naturally for 15 minutes and then quick-release the remaining pressure. Transfer the lamb steaks to a cutting board with a slotted spoon. Shred the meat with two forks, discarding the bones and fat.

5   Select **SAUTÉ** and adjust to **NORMAL/MEDIUM** heat. When the liquid comes to a simmer, liquid fat will pool on the top around the edges of the pot. Spoon this off and discard. Return the meat to the pot and season the sauce with salt and black pepper. Press **CANCEL**. Serve the sauce garnished with the cheese and mint.

The sauce can be stored in an airtight container in the refrigerator for up to 5 days or in the freezer for up to 3 months. Reheat gently before serving.

VEGGIE LOVER'S PASTA SAUCE

This vegetable-packed sauce is chunky, so it's best served over sturdy pasta shapes like rigatoni, ziti, or penne. The recipe is adaptable—you can leave out any vegetables you don't like, but be sure to replace them with ones that you *do* enjoy to retain the moisture ratio so the pot will pressurize.

1	medium (10-ounce) eggplant, cut into 1-inch cubes
	Salt and pepper
3	tablespoons olive oil
1	medium yellow onion, chopped
1	green bell pepper, seeded and chopped
6	ounces cremini mushrooms, sliced
1½	teaspoons dried oregano
3	medium garlic cloves, finely chopped
2	tablespoons tomato paste
1	(28-ounce) can whole peeled San Marzano tomatoes, chopped (see Note, page 192), with their juices
1½	cups plain frozen artichoke hearts (5 ounces; do not use marinated artichokes)

1 Toss the eggplant with the salt in a colander and set aside for 15 minutes. Pat the eggplant dry with paper towels to absorb the bitter juices. Set aside.

2 Put the oil in the pot, select **SAUTÉ**, and adjust to **MORE/HIGH** heat. When the oil is hot, add the onion, bell pepper, mushrooms, oregano, and ½ teaspoon salt and cook until the vegetables are just tender, 4 minutes. Add the garlic and tomato paste and cook until fragrant, 45 seconds. Press **CANCEL**.

3 Add the eggplant and the tomatoes with their juices and stir to combine. Place the artichoke hearts on top of the sauce but don't stir them in; this will help them retain their shape while cooking. Lock on the lid, select the **PRESSURE COOK** function, and adjust to **HIGH** pressure for 15 minutes. Make sure the steam valve is in the "Sealing" position and that the "Keep Warm" button is off.

4 When the cooking time is up, let the pressure come down naturally for 15 minutes and then quick-release the remaining pressure. Season with salt and black pepper.

The sauce can be stored in an airtight container in the refrigerator for up to 5 days. It does not freeze well.

RIGATONI ALLA VODKA

Serves 4 | **Active time: 10 minutes** | **Total time: 35 minutes**

The provenance of this comforting pasta dish spiked with vodka is debated, but that hasn't stopped it from becoming a popular Italian-American restaurant staple. The thinking is that the vodka tenderizes the tomatoes. Don't worry, you can't taste the alcohol—all you'll detect is a delicious, creamy sauce with a little bit of heat. If you like spicy food, try using pepper-infused vodka for an extra kick.

2   tablespoons unsalted butter

3   medium garlic cloves, sliced

2   tablespoons tomato paste

1   (14.5-ounce) can crushed tomatoes

¼   cup vodka

12   ounces dry (uncooked) rigatoni pasta

    Pinch of red chile flakes

    Salt and pepper

½   cup heavy cream

½   cup grated Pecorino Romano cheese

½   cup fresh basil leaves, torn into small pieces

1. Put the butter in the pot, select **SAUTÉ**, and adjust to **NORMAL/ MEDIUM** heat. When the butter has melted, add the garlic and cook until fragrant, 45 seconds. Add the tomato paste and cook, stirring frequently, until it begins to brown, 1 minute. Add the tomatoes and vodka and simmer for 1 minute to boil off some of the alcohol. Press **CANCEL**.

2. Add the rigatoni, red chile flakes, 2½ cups cold water, 1 teaspoon salt, and several grinds of black pepper. Lock on the lid, select the **PRESSURE COOK** function, and adjust to **LOW** pressure for 6 minutes. Make sure the steam valve is in the "Sealing" position and that the "Keep Warm" button is off.

3. When the cooking time is up, quick-release the pressure. Remove the lid. Add the cream and stir to combine. Let the pasta stand in the pot, uncovered, for 5 minutes, stirring occasionally, to allow the sauce to thicken. Stir the cheese and basil into the pasta and season with salt and black pepper.

PENNE WITH FRESH TUNA AND CHERRY TOMATOES

Serves 4   Active time: 5 minutes   Total time: 30 minutes

In this Southern Italian–inspired one-pot pasta, a thick tuna steak cooks to moist perfection at the same time as the penne, cherry tomatoes, and olives. When the cooking is done, break up the tuna into large flakes with a spoon and mix it into the pasta. The sauce will look thin at first glance, but it thickens into a beautiful, clingy sauce upon standing.

12	ounces dry (uncooked) penne pasta
2	cups cherry tomatoes, halved
1	small sweet onion, halved lengthwise and thinly sliced through the root end (about 1 cup)
⅓	cup oil-cured olives, pitted and halved
3	tablespoons olive oil
4	medium garlic cloves, thinly sliced
¼	teaspoon red chile flakes
	Salt and pepper
1	(8-ounce) tuna steak, about 1½ inches thick
½	cup fresh basil leaves
1½	teaspoons finely grated lemon zest
2	tablespoons fresh lemon juice

1 Combine the pasta, cherry tomatoes, onion, olives, oil, garlic, red chile flakes, ½ teaspoon salt, and several grinds of black pepper in the pot. Add 2¾ cups water and stir to combine. Place the tuna on top of the pasta mixture but do not submerge it.

2 Lock on the lid, select the **PRESSURE COOK** function, and adjust to **LOW** pressure for 6 minutes. Make sure the steam valve is in the "Sealing" position and that the "Keep Warm" button is off.

3 While the pasta is cooking, stack the basil leaves, roll them up tightly as you would a sleeping bag, and slice crosswise into thin ribbons.

4 When the cooking time is up, quick-release the pressure. Remove the lid. Add the basil, lemon zest, and lemon juice to the pot and stir, breaking up the fish into bite-size chunks. Season with salt and black pepper. Let the pasta stand in the pot set in the appliance, uncovered, for 5 minutes to allow the sauce to thicken before serving.

⬢ FARFALLE WITH SAUSAGE MEATBALLS, SUN-DRIED TOMATOES, AND ARUGULA

Serves 4 | Active time: 20 minutes | Total time: 35 minutes

This lovely pasta is made up of ingredients you probably already have in your kitchen, so it's sure to become a go-to on busy weeknights. The recipe is endlessly adaptable—make it lighter by using turkey sausage; substitute chopped dandelion greens, escarole, or baby kale for the arugula; or use jarred roasted red peppers instead of the sun-dried tomatoes.

8 ounces bulk sweet Italian pork sausage

1 tablespoon olive oil

12 ounces dry (uncooked) farfalle pasta

2 cups Homemade Chicken Broth (page 198) or low-sodium store-bought broth

1 small yellow onion, halved lengthwise and thinly sliced through the root end (about 1 cup)

½ cup oil-packed sun-dried tomatoes, drained and chopped

4 medium garlic cloves, thinly sliced

1 teaspoon fennel seeds

1 teaspoon dried Italian seasoning

Salt and pepper

2 cups loosely packed baby arugula leaves

½ cup grated Pecorino Romano cheese

1 Form the sausage into dabs that are about 1 tablespoon each—no need to roll them into perfect spheres (rustic is good). Put the oil in the pot, select **SAUTÉ**, and adjust to **NORMAL/MEDIUM** heat. When the oil is hot, add the sausage dabs and cook them, without stirring, for a few minutes. Stir gently and cook until browned on a second side; they don't need to be cooked through, as they'll finish cooking with the pasta. Press **CANCEL**.

2 Pour off all but 1 tablespoon of the fat in the pot. Add the pasta, broth, onion, sun-dried tomatoes, garlic, fennel seeds, Italian seasoning, ½ teaspoon salt, several grinds of pepper, and 1 cup cold water. Stir to combine.

3 Lock on the lid, select the **PRESSURE COOK** function, and adjust to **LOW** pressure for 6 minutes. Make sure the steam valve is in the "Sealing" position and that the "Keep Warm" button is off.

4 When the cooking time is up, quick-release the pressure. Remove the lid, stir, and let the pasta stand in the pot, uncovered, for 5 minutes to allow the sauce to thicken. Add the arugula and cheese and stir to combine. Season with salt and pepper.

ORECCHIETTE WITH BROCCOLI RABE

Serves 4 | **Active time: 10 minutes** | **Total time: 30 minutes**

Orecchio means "ear" in Italian, a nod to the concave shape of this round pasta. Orecchiette serve as perfect little catcher's mitts for this easy, zesty sauce of garlic, anchovies, and peppery broccoli rabe (also known as broccoli raab or rapini). If you're not a fan of the bitterness of rabe, substitute broccolini or broccoli. Crème fraîche is stirred into the pasta at the end of cooking to make a tantalizingly creamy sauce with just the right tang.

2   tablespoons olive oil

1   large shallot, thinly sliced

5   garlic cloves, chopped

3   anchovies

1   pound dry (uncooked) orecchiette pasta

3   cups Homemade Chicken or Vegetable Broth (page 198 or 201) or low-sodium store-bought broth

Pinch of red chile flakes

Salt and pepper

8   ounces broccoli rabe or broccolini, cut into 2-inch pieces

½   cup crème fraîche or sour cream

½   cup grated Pecorino Romano cheese

1 Put the oil in the pot, select **SAUTÉ**, and adjust to **NORMAL/MEDIUM** heat. When the oil is hot, add the shallot, garlic, and anchovies and cook, stirring occasionally, until the shallot is tender and the garlic is fragrant but not browned, 3 minutes. Press **CANCEL**.

2 Add the pasta, broth, red chile flakes, 1 cup cold water, ½ teaspoon salt, and several grinds of black pepper and stir so the pasta is mostly submerged. Place the broccoli rabe on top of the pasta mixture, but do not stir.

3 Lock on the lid, select the **PRESSURE COOK** function, and adjust to **LOW** pressure for 5 minutes. Make sure the steam valve is in the "Sealing" position and that the "Keep Warm" button is off.

4 When the cooking time is up, quick-release the pressure. Remove the lid, add the crème fraîche and cheese, and stir to combine. Season with salt and black pepper. Transfer the mixture to a serving dish and let stand for 5 minutes before serving to allow the sauce to thicken slightly.

SHRIMP SCAMPI LINGUINE

Serves 4 | **Active time: 15 minutes** | **Total time: 40 minutes**

Raw shrimp are too delicate to cook in an Instant Pot, but frozen shrimp cook perfectly in 6 minutes. In this lovely, light dish, they cook right along with the linguine and garlic-lemon sauce. For best results, buy large shrimp, labeled "extra jumbo" or "16/20," which refers to the number of shrimp per pound.

2 tablespoons olive oil

3 tablespoons unsalted butter

½ medium yellow onion, finely chopped (¾ cup)

2 teaspoons chopped fresh oregano, or 1 teaspoon dried

5 medium garlic cloves, thinly sliced

½ cup dry vermouth or dry white wine

12 ounces dry (uncooked) linguine, broken in half

1½ cups Homemade Seafood or Chicken Broth (page 200 or 198) or low-sodium store-bought broth

Pinch of red chile flakes

Salt and pepper

1¼ pounds large (16/20-count) frozen peeled and deveined shrimp

¼ cup chopped fresh Italian parsley

1½ teaspoons finely grated lemon zest

2 tablespoons fresh lemon juice

1 Put the oil and butter in the pot, select **SAUTÉ**, and adjust to **NORMAL/ MEDIUM** heat. When the butter has melted, add the onion and oregano and cook, stirring frequently, until tender, 4 minutes. Add the garlic and cook until fragrant, 45 seconds. Add the vermouth and simmer for 1 minute to burn off some of the alcohol. Press **CANCEL**.

2 Add the linguine, broth, red chile flakes, 1½ cups hot water, ½ teaspoon salt, and several grinds of black pepper. Stir to combine, making sure most of the pasta is submerged. Place the frozen shrimp on top of the pasta mixture, but don't stir them into the sauce. Lock on the lid, select the **PRESSURE COOK** function, and adjust to **LOW** pressure for 5 minutes. Make sure the steam valve is in the "Sealing" position and that the "Keep Warm" button is off.

3 When the cooking time is up, quick-release the pressure. Remove the lid and add the parsley, lemon zest, and lemon juice to the pot. Stir with tongs, breaking up any clumped pasta and submerging it in the sauce. Season with salt and lots of black pepper. Let the pasta stand in the pot for 5 minutes to allow the sauce to thicken before serving.

🍲 SPAGHETTI CARBONARA

Serves 4 | **Active time: 15 minutes** | **Total time: 30 minutes**

This rich Roman pasta dish is the ultimate weeknight comfort food.
The spaghetti is cooked under pressure with broth, pancetta, and garlic first,
and then the dish is finished by tossing the mixture with beaten eggs, cheese,
and parsley in a big serving bowl. The heat of the pasta and cooking liquid cooks
the eggs just enough to create a velvety sauce that perfectly coats the pasta.

3	tablespoons olive oil
⅓	cup diced pancetta, from a ½-inch-thick slab, or chopped thick-cut bacon
5	medium garlic cloves, thinly sliced
½	cup dry vermouth or dry white wine
12	ounces dry (uncooked) spaghetti, broken in half
1½	cups Homemade Chicken or Vegetable Broth (page 198 or 201) or low-sodium store-bought broth
	Salt and pepper
3	large eggs, beaten
½	cup finely grated Parmesan cheese
¼	cup chopped fresh Italian parsley

1 Put the oil in the pot, select **SAUTÉ**, and adjust to **NORMAL/MEDIUM** heat. When the oil is hot, add the pancetta and cook, stirring frequently, until it begins to brown, 3 minutes. Add the garlic and cook until fragrant, 45 seconds. Add the wine and cook for 1 minute to burn off some of the alcohol. Press **CANCEL**.

2 Add the spaghetti, broth, 1½ cups hot water, ½ teaspoon salt, and several grinds of pepper and stir to combine, making sure most of the pasta is submerged. Lock on the lid, select the **PRESSURE COOK** function, and adjust to **LOW** pressure for 5 minutes. Make sure the steam valve is in the "Sealing" position and that the "Keep Warm" button is off.

3 While the pasta is cooking, in a large, wide serving bowl, whisk together the eggs, cheese, and parsley. Set aside.

4 When the cooking time is up, quick-release the pressure. Remove the lid and stir the mixture with tongs, separating any clumped pasta. Pour the mixture into the serving bowl with the egg mixture and toss with tongs to coat the pasta. Season with salt and pepper. Serve right away.

RAVIOLI WITH SAUSAGE SAUCE

Serves 4 Active time: 15 minutes Total time: 40 minutes

I always have a bag of cheese ravioli stashed in the freezer for quick meals. With my Instant Pot, it's an even quicker process because I can throw the frozen ravioli right into the sauce and pressure cook them together—no waiting around for water to boil.

1 tablespoon olive oil

8 ounces bulk Italian pork sausage

3 cups Homemade Marinara (page 192), or 1 (24-ounce) jar marinara sauce

1 cup Homemade Chicken or Beef Broth (page 198 or 199) or low-sodium store-bought broth

Salt and pepper

25 ounces frozen cheese ravioli

¼ cup chopped fresh basil leaves

1 Put the oil in the pot, select **SAUTÉ**, and adjust to **MORE/HIGH** heat. When the oil is hot, add the sausage and cook, stirring frequently to break up the meat, until cooked through and browned, 5 minutes. Add the marinara sauce broth, ½ teaspoon salt, and several grinds of black pepper and stir to combine. Bring to a simmer and cook, stirring frequently, for 5 minutes. Press **CANCEL**.

2 Add the frozen ravioli to the pot, arranging them in an even layer; do not stir. Lock on the lid, select the **PRESSURE COOK** function, and adjust to **HIGH** pressure for 2 minutes. Make sure the steam valve is in the "Sealing" position and that the "Keep Warm" button is off.

3 When the cooking time is up, let the pressure come down naturally, about 10 minutes. Transfer the ravioli to a large serving bowl. Depending on the thickness and sugar content of the marinara you use, you may find a small amount of browned sauce at the bottom of the Instant Pot. Stir it into the rest of the marinara to incorporate it before serving. Pour the sauce over the ravioli and sprinkle with the basil before serving.

CREAMY BUTTERNUT AND KALE LASAGNA

Serves 4   Active time: 15 minutes   Total time: 1 hour 10 minutes

Dairy products curdle when cooked under pressure if they're placed directly in the Instant Pot, but the dairy in this creamy lasagna is protected by using the "pot in a pot" method: The lasagna is layered in a pan and set on a trivet over water in the pot for a more gentle approach. The no-cook white sauce, a combo of cream cheese and milk, comes together in seconds in a blender, and precooked butternut squash and frozen kale make this recipe a cinch to throw together.

1   **(8-ounce) package cream cheese, at room temperature**

½   **cup whole or 2% milk**

¼   **teaspoon granulated garlic**

⅛   **teaspoon freshly grated nutmeg**

Pinch of cayenne pepper

1   **cup grated part-skim mozzarella cheese**

½   **cup grated Fontina cheese**

6 to 9   **oven-ready lasagna sheets (about 3 ounces)**

1½   **cups Butternut Squash with Rosemary (page 166) or defrosted frozen squash**

1   **(8-ounce) bag frozen kale, defrosted and squeezed dry**

1 In a blender, combine the cream cheese, milk, garlic powder, nutmeg, and cayenne and blend until smooth. In a medium bowl, toss together the mozzarella and Fontina cheeses; set aside.

2 Spray an 8-inch springform pan with cooking spray. Arrange about 2½ noodles in an even layer on the bottom of the pan, breaking them to fit. Spoon ½ cup of the sauce over the noodles and top with half the squash and kale. Sprinkle with ½ cup of the cheese mixture.

3 Arrange another layer of noodles in the pan, spoon about ½ cup of the sauce over them, and then lay the remaining vegetables over the top. Sprinkle with ½ cup of the cheese mixture. Arrange a final layer of noodles over the top. Cover with the remaining sauce and sprinkle with the remaining cheese mixture. Cover the lasagna tightly with foil. Place the pan on a trivet with handles.

4 Pour 1½ cups cold water into the pot. Lower the lasagna on the trivet into the pot. Lock on the lid, select the **PRESSURE COOK** function, and adjust to **HIGH** pressure for 40 minutes. Make sure the steam valve is in the "Sealing" position and that the "Keep Warm" button is off.

5 When the cooking time is up, let the pressure come down naturally for 10 minutes and then quick-release the remaining pressure. Remove the lid and blot the foil with paper towels to remove any moisture.

6 Lift the lasagna out of the appliance and uncover. If you'd like the top to be browned, set the uncovered lasagna on a baking sheet and broil until the cheeses are golden brown, about 3 minutes. Place the pan on a large dinner plate and let the lasagna stand for 5 minutes before unlocking and removing the sides of the pan. Cut the lasagna into wedges to serve.

SAUSAGE LASAGNA

Serves 4 | Active time: 20 minutes | Total time: 1 hour

This recipe is the perfect solution when you crave layered, gooey, oven-baked lasagna goodness but don't want to turn the oven on. Use flat, no-boil lasagna noodles for best results; noodles with ruffled edges are difficult to fit in the pan. If you'd like to make this lasagna meatless, substitute 8 ounces chopped vegetarian Italian sausage for the pork.

1 tablespoon olive oil

10 ounces bulk Italian pork sausage

1 cup Homemade Ricotta (page 194) or store-bought

1 large egg

2 tablespoons chopped fresh basil

¼ teaspoon freshly grated nutmeg

Salt and pepper

6 to 9 oven-ready lasagna sheets (about 3 ounces)

1⅔ cups Homemade Marinara (page 192) or jarred marinara sauce

1 cup grated mozzarella cheese

¼ cup grated Parmesan cheese

1 Put the oil in the pot, select **SAUTÉ**, and adjust to **MORE/HIGH** heat. When the oil is hot, add the sausage and cook, stirring occasionally and breaking up the meat with a wooden spoon, until browned, 5 minutes. Add ¼ cup cold water and scrape up the browned bits from the bottom of the pan. Press **CANCEL**. Transfer the meat to a colander to drain off the fat and liquid. Wipe out the pot with a paper towel. Add 1½ cups hot water to the pot.

2 In a medium bowl, mix the ricotta, egg, basil, and nutmeg with a fork until blended. Season with salt and pepper.

3 Spray an 8-inch springform pan with cooking spray. Place 2 noodles in an even layer on the bottom of the pan, breaking them to fit. Spoon ½ cup of the sauce over the noodles and scatter with half the sausage and ⅓ cup of the mozzarella. Arrange another layer of noodles in the pan, spoon ⅔ cup of the sauce over them, then dollop all the ricotta over the sauce.

4 Arrange another layer of noodles over the ricotta and spoon the remaining sausage and remaining sauce over the top. Sprinkle the remaining mozzarella and all the Parmesan over the top.

5 Cover the pan tightly with foil and place it on a trivet with handles. Lower the lasagna into the pot. Lock on the lid, select the **PRESSURE COOK** function, and adjust to **HIGH** pressure for 30 minutes. Make sure the steam valve is in the "Sealing" position and that the "Keep Warm" button is off.

6 When the cooking time is up, let the pressure come down naturally for 10 minutes and then quick-release the remaining pressure. Remove the lid and blot the foil with paper towels to remove any moisture.

7 Lift the lasagna out of the appliance and uncover. If you'd like the top of the lasagna to be browned, set the uncovered lasagna on a baking sheet and broil until the cheeses are golden brown, about 3 minutes. Place the pan on a large dinner plate, unlock, and remove the sides of the pan. Cut into wedges to serve.

ONE POT FARRO RISOTTO WITH WILD MUSHROOMS

Serves 4   Active time: 18 minutes   Total time: 1 hour 10 minutes

Nutty semi-pearled farro behaves like Arborio rice in this recipe, releasing starch as it cooks to make a creamy, earthy, risotto-like dish. Unlike Arborio rice, semi-pearled farro still retains a distinctive chew and is full of healthy fiber. The dish is an excellent vegetarian main dish, but it's also ideal as a side dish for roasted chicken, pork, or beef.

2 tablespoons olive oil

1 large leek, light green and white parts only, halved lengthwise, rinsed well, and chopped

12 ounces wild mushrooms, trimmed and sliced

1 tablespoon chopped fresh sage, or 1½ teaspoons dried

2 teaspoons chopped fresh rosemary

Salt and pepper

1½ cups semi-pearled farro

3 medium garlic cloves, chopped

½ cup dry red wine, such as Chianti

2½ cups Homemade Chicken or Vegetable Broth (page 198 or 201) or low-sodium store-bought broth

1 (2-inch) Parmesan cheese rind (optional)

½ cup grated Parmesan cheese, plus more for garnish

1 Put the oil in the pot, select **SAUTÉ**, and adjust to **NORMAL/MEDIUM** heat. When the oil is hot, add the leek, mushrooms, sage, rosemary, ½ teaspoon salt, and a few grinds of pepper. Cook, stirring frequently, until the mushrooms have released their liquid and are beginning to brown, 8 minutes. Add the farro and garlic and cook, stirring frequently, for 1 minute. Add the wine and cook for 1 minute to burn off some of the alcohol. Press **CANCEL**.

2 Add the broth and cheese rind (if using) and stir to combine. Lock on the lid, select the **PRESSURE COOK** function, and adjust to **HIGH** pressure for 8 minutes. Make sure the steam valve is in the "Sealing" position and that the "Keep Warm" button is off.

3 When the cooking time is up, let the pressure come down naturally for 10 minutes and then quick-release the remaining pressure. Discard the cheese rind. Stir the cheese into the risotto and season with salt and pepper. Let the risotto rest for 5 minutes in the appliance; it will thicken as it stands. Pass additional grated cheese at the table.

SCALLOP, FENNEL, AND PROSECCO RISOTTO

Serves 4 | Active time: 15 minutes | Total time: 40 minutes

Creamy risotto made with fennel, Prosecco, and lemon sets the perfect flavor stage for spice-crusted seared scallops in this light seafood dish. Be sure to buy "dry packed" scallops rather than "wet," which are treated with sodium tripolyphosphates and will exude liquid as they cook, yielding soggy scallops. For a shortcut, instead of searing the scallops separately, add chopped raw diver scallops or thriftier bay scallops to the risotto after lifting the lid and simmer them for a few minutes, until they are just cooked.

1   **medium (8-ounce) fennel bulb with fronds**

2   **tablespoons olive oil**

1   **medium yellow onion, finely chopped**

1   **cup Arborio rice**

1   **cup Prosecco**

2   **cups Homemade Seafood Broth (page 200) or low-sodium store-bought broth**

12   **large diver scallops (about 1 pound)**

1   **teaspoon fennel seeds, ground in a spice grinder or mortar and pestle**

    Salt and pepper

1   **tablespoon safflower oil**

1   **teaspoon finely grated lemon zest**

2   **tablespoons fresh lemon juice**

1. Cut the feathery fronds away from the fennel, chop, and set aside. Cut out the core and discard; finely chop the bulb. Put the olive oil in the pot, select **SAUTÉ**, and adjust to **NORMAL/MEDIUM** heat. When the oil is hot, add the onion and fennel bulb and cook, stirring occasionally, until tender, 6 minutes. Add the rice and cook, stirring continuously, for 1 minute. Add the wine and simmer for 1 minute to burn off some of the alcohol. Add the broth and select **CANCEL**.

2. Lock on the lid, select the **PRESSURE COOK** function, and adjust to **HIGH** pressure for 8 minutes. Make sure the steam valve is in the "Sealing" position and that the "Keep Warm" button is off.

3. While the risotto cooks, heat a heavy cast-iron skillet or sauté pan over medium-high heat until very hot but not smoking. Pat the scallops dry and sprinkle with the fennel seeds, then season with salt and pepper. Drizzle the scallops with the safflower oil and put them in the pan. Cook until browned on one side, 3 minutes. Turn the scallops over, reduce the heat to medium, and cook until the scallops are white and opaque in the center, 1 to 2 minutes, depending on size. Transfer to a plate.

4. When the risotto cooking time is up, quick-release the pressure. Stir in the fennel fronds, lemon zest, and lemon juice. Season with salt and pepper. Divide the risotto among four shallow bowls and top with the seared scallops.

HERBED POLENTA

The Instant Pot makes perfect polenta without the laborious stirring stovetop polenta recipes require. The gentle heat of cooking on low pressure means you'll get smooth, creamy polenta that won't stick to the bottom of the pot. The blend of parsley, sage, rosemary, and thyme gives this soft polenta a woodsy flavor that lends itself to being served alongside hearty meat dishes like pot roast and braised lamb.

2 tablespoons unsalted butter

1 large shallot, finely chopped

2 teaspoons chopped fresh sage leaves

2 teaspoons chopped fresh rosemary

2 teaspoons chopped fresh thyme leaves

4 cups Homemade Chicken or Vegetable Broth (page 198 or 201) or low-sodium store-bought broth

Salt

1 cup polenta (not quick-cooking)

½ cup grated Parmesan cheese

¼ cup milk

3 tablespoons chopped fresh Italian parsley

¼ teaspoon freshly grated nutmeg

Pepper

1. Place the butter in the pot, select **SAUTÉ**, and adjust to **MORE/HIGH** heat. When the butter has melted, add the shallot, sage, rosemary, and thyme and cook, stirring frequently, until the shallot is tender, 4 minutes. Add the broth and ½ teaspoon salt. When the liquid comes to a simmer, gradually whisk in the polenta. Press **CANCEL**.

2. Lock on the lid, select the **PRESSURE COOK** function, and adjust to **LOW** pressure for 8 minutes. Make sure the steam valve is in the "Sealing" position and that the "Keep Warm" button is off.

3. When the cooking time is up, let the pressure come down naturally for 15 minutes and then quick-release the remaining pressure. Unlock the lid and remove the pot from the appliance. Stir in the cheese, milk, parsley, and nutmeg. Season with salt and pepper.

4. Serve immediately as soft polenta, or transfer it to a container and refrigerate until solid. To reheat solid polenta, cut it into 1-inch-thick slabs and sauté them in olive oil in a nonstick pan over medium-high heat until crispy, 3 minutes per side.

Solid polenta can be refrigerated, tightly wrapped in plastic, for up to 5 days.

RED WINE RISOTTO WITH ITALIAN SAUSAGE

ONE POT

Serves 4   Active time: 20 minutes   Total time: 50 minutes

Dry Italian red wine like Nebbiolo or Chianti is ideal for this comforting wine-infused risotto. Adding julienned radicchio to the rice along with the cheese at the end of cooking adds a slight bitterness that is a nice counterpoint to the rich sausage, but it's an optional step.

8   ounces bulk mild Italian pork sausage

2   tablespoons olive oil

1   medium red onion, chopped

2   teaspoons finely chopped fresh rosemary

3   medium garlic cloves, finely chopped

1   tablespoon tomato paste

1½ cups Arborio rice

2   cups dry Italian red wine, such as Nebbiolo or Chianti

2   cups Homemade Chicken or Vegetable Broth (page 198 or 201) or low-sodium store-bought broth

½   cup grated Asiago cheese

1   (6-ounce) head radicchio, cored and thinly sliced (optional)

Salt and pepper

1 Form the sausage into dabs that are about 2 teaspoons each—no need to roll them into perfect spheres (rustic is good). Put the oil in the pot, select **SAUTÉ**, and adjust to **NORMAL/MEDIUM** heat. When the oil is hot, add the sausage dabs and cook, without stirring, for a few minutes. Stir gently and cook until browned on a second side, 2 minutes; they don't need to be cooked through, as they'll finish cooking in the risotto. Remove the sausage from the pot with a slotted spoon.

2 Add the onion and rosemary to the pot and cook, stirring frequently, until the onion is tender, 4 minutes. Add the garlic and tomato paste and cook until fragrant, 45 seconds. Add the rice and stir to coat with the aromatics. Add the wine and simmer for 1 minute to burn off some of the alcohol. Press **CANCEL**.

3 Add the broth and return the sausage to the pot. Lock on the lid, select the **PRESSURE COOK** function, and adjust to **HIGH** pressure for 7 minutes. Make sure the steam valve is in the "Sealing" position and that the "Keep Warm" button is off.

4 When the cooking time is up, let the pressure come down naturally for 10 minutes and then quick-release the remaining pressure. Stir the cheese and radicchio into the risotto and season with salt and pepper.

RISOTTO PRIMAVERA

ONE POT

Serves 4   Active time: 15 minutes   Total time: 45 minutes

This light, creamy risotto, packed with asparagus, fresh fava beans, spinach, and lemon, is just the thing to celebrate the arrival of spring. If you can only find thick asparagus, slice the stalks in half lengthwise before cutting them up so they cook through in the brief amount of time they are simmered with the rice.

2 tablespoons olive oil

1 small sweet onion, chopped (about 1 cup)

2 teaspoons chopped fresh thyme, or ½ teaspoon dried

1 cup Arborio rice

½ cup dry vermouth or dry white wine

3 cups Homemade Chicken or Vegetable Broth (page 198 or 201) or low-sodium store-bought broth

8 ounces asparagus, tough ends snapped off and discarded, stalks cut into 1-inch pieces

1 cup peeled fresh or frozen fava beans or peas

2 cups baby spinach leaves

½ cup grated Parmesan cheese

1 teaspoon finely grated lemon zest

1 tablespoon fresh lemon juice

Salt and pepper

1 Put the oil in the pot, select **SAUTÉ**, and adjust to **NORMAL/MEDIUM** heat. When the oil is hot, add the onion and thyme and cook, stirring occasionally, until tender, 4 minutes. Add the rice and cook, stirring continuously, for 1 minute. Add the vermouth and simmer for 1 minute to burn off some of the alcohol. Press **CANCEL**.

2 Add the broth, stir to combine, and lock on the lid. Select the **PRESSURE COOK** function and adjust to **HIGH** pressure for 8 minutes. Make sure the steam valve is in the "Sealing" position and that the "Keep Warm" button is off.

3 When the time is up, quick-release the pressure and remove the lid. Add the asparagus and fava beans or peas. Select **SAUTÉ** and adjust to **NORMAL/MEDIUM** heat. Cook, uncovered, stirring occasionally, until the vegetables are crisp-tender, 3 minutes. Add a bit of water while cooking, if necessary, to keep the risotto loose and saucy. Add the spinach, cheese, lemon zest, and lemon juice and stir to combine. Press **CANCEL**. Season with salt and pepper.

POLENTA WITH BROCCOLI AND SMOKED MOZZARELLA

Serves 4 to 6 | Active time: 2 minutes | Total time: 30 minutes

I first had this amazing broccoli-and-cheese polenta dish in an unlikely spot—a macrobiotic cafeteria in Urbino, Italy. Their version was cooked for hours in a great big pot until the broccoli fell apart into tiny flecks in the creamy polenta. The Instant Pot makes it easy to arrive at the same creamy goodness in minutes, not hours. Serve the polenta soft as a side dish for saucy braises, or chill until solid and sauté slices, as pictured here, to serve alongside roasted meats or grilled vegetables.

4 cups Homemade Chicken or Vegetable Broth (page 198 or 201) or low-sodium store-bought broth

2 tablespoons extra-virgin olive oil or unsalted butter

Salt

1 bay leaf

1 cup whole-grain polenta (not quick-cooking)

1 large (6- to 8-ounce) broccoli crown

1 cup grated smoked mozzarella or scamorza cheese

Pepper

1 Place the broth, oil, ½ teaspoon salt, and the bay leaf in the pot. Select **SAUTÉ** and adjust to **MORE/HIGH** heat. When the broth comes to a simmer, gradually whisk in the polenta. Press **CANCEL**.

2 Place the whole broccoli crown in the pot, stem-side down. Lock on the lid, select the **PRESSURE COOK** function, and adjust to **LOW** pressure for 8 minutes. Make sure the steam valve is in the "Sealing" position and that the "Keep Warm" button is off.

3 When the cooking time is up, let the pressure come down naturally for 10 minutes and then quick-release the remaining pressure. Unlock the lid and remove the pot from the appliance. Stir in the cheese with a wooden spoon, breaking up the broccoli into bite-size pieces as you stir. Season with salt and pepper.

4 Serve immediately as soft polenta, or transfer it to a container and refrigerate until solid. To reheat solid polenta, cut it into 1-inch-thick slabs and sauté them in olive oil in a nonstick pan over medium-high heat until crispy, 3 minutes per side.

Solid polenta can be refrigerated, tightly wrapped in plastic, for up to 5 days.

POULTRY

Chicken is a go-to ingredient for home cooks everywhere, and Italy is no exception. In this chapter, you'll find recipes including a juicy, whole "roasted" chicken with crispy skin, saucy cacciatore, and quick yet elegant mozzarella-and-basil-stuffed chicken breasts with balsamic pan sauce.

Chicken is a lean meat by nature, so it's important to follow the recipes here closely to avoid overcooking, especially paying attention to the weight of the chicken parts in the ingredients list. Chickens breasts in particular vary wildly in size—boneless, skinless chicken breasts range in weight from 6 ounces for very small breasts to up to 1 pound for enormous ones, so try to get as close as possible to the size specified for the best results. Since chicken thighs are less lean, there's more leeway in size and cooking time.

Turkey breasts are great when cooked in the Instant Pot, too. Just be sure to buy good-quality turkey that has not been injected with saline solutions—those artificially add water weight (and cost you more) without any other benefit. I call for boneless turkey breast halves with the skin on to help keep the lean meat moist. Test the temperature of the turkey breast with an instant-read thermometer at the end of cooking and keep in mind that the meat will finish cooking as it rests.

The term *poultry* doesn't cover just chicken and turkey. I've also included a delicious recipe for duck ragù I learned in the Veneto region. Duck legs melt beautifully into a rich tomato sauce in the Instant Pot. It's a lovely spin on the classic beef ragù, and it's just begging to be tossed with fresh pasta.

PESTO ROASTED CHICKEN

Serves 4 to 6 | Active time: 10 minutes | Total time: 1 hour 10 minutes

A whole chicken comes out of the Instant Pot tender and juicy in just 28 minutes. Sliding pesto (or another spice paste of your choice) under the skin of the bird has multiple benefits—it adds loads of flavor, helps keep the breast meat moist, and enhances the cooking liquid so you can use it to make a delicious pan sauce. Be sure to get a bird that is as close to 4 pounds as possible—a smaller chicken may overcook, and a larger bird won't fit in the pot.

1   (4-pound) whole roasting chicken, neck and giblets in cavity removed

½   cup Homemade Pesto (page 193) or store-bought pesto

    Salt and pepper

1   cup Homemade Chicken Broth (page 198) or low-sodium store-bought broth

2   medium garlic cloves, thinly sliced

1   bay leaf

1 Loosen the skin covering the breast and thighs of the chicken by carefully sliding your fingers under the skin, taking care not to tear the skin covering the top of the bird. Slide the pesto under the skin of the chicken, pressing to distribute it evenly over the breast and thighs. Tuck the wings behind the chicken's back and tie the drumsticks together with butcher's twine. Season the outside of the chicken liberally with salt and pepper.

2 Place a trivet with handles in the pot and add the broth, garlic, and bay leaf. Place the chicken breast-side up on the trivet. Lock on the lid, select the **PRESSURE COOK** function, and adjust to **HIGH** pressure for 28 minutes. Make sure the steam valve is in the "Sealing" position and that the "Keep Warm" button is off.

3 When the cooking time is up, quick-release the pressure. Unlock the lid and insert an instant-read thermometer into the center of the thickest part of the breast; it should register 160°F; the thigh should register 175°F. If the chicken is not done, cover with a regular pot lid, select **SAUTÉ**, and adjust to **NORMAL/MEDIUM** heat for 5 minutes. Check the temperature again.

4 If crispy skin is desired, preheat the broiler and adjust the oven rack so that it is 8 inches below the broiler element. Line a rimmed baking sheet with foil.

5 Place the chicken on the prepared baking sheet and broil until the skin is browned, about 3 minutes. Transfer the chicken to a cutting board, tent with foil, and let it rest for 10 minutes.

6 While the chicken rests, reduce the cooking liquid in the pot. Select **SAUTÉ** and adjust to **MORE/HIGH** heat. Simmer, stirring occasionally, until the liquid has reduced by half, about 5 minutes. Press **CANCEL**. Discard the bay leaf. Carve the chicken and serve with the sauce.

STUFFED CAPRESE CHICKEN BREASTS

Serves 4   Active time: 20 minutes   Total time: 40 minutes

All the things you love about Caprese salads—gooey fresh mozzarella, ripe tomatoes,
and basil—are stuffed into chicken breasts in this easy weeknight meal. The cooking liquid,
thickened with a little butter and flour and flavored with a little balsamic vinegar,
becomes a rich, piquant gravy. Serve this comforting dish with Truffled
Celery Root Mashers (page 165) or Herbed Polenta (page 97).

4   small (8-ounce) boneless,
     skinless chicken
     breast halves

     Salt and pepper

1   (8-ounce) ball fresh
     mozzarella cheese,
     thickly sliced

1½   Roma (plum) tomatoes,
     sliced

½   cup fresh basil leaves,
     left whole

4   slices prosciutto

1   tablespoon olive oil

⅔   cup Homemade Chicken
     Broth (page 198) or
     low-sodium store-
     bought broth

2   tablespoons balsamic
     vinegar

1   tablespoon all-purpose
     flour

1   tablespoon unsalted
     butter, at room
     temperature

1 With a sharp boning knife, cut a horizontal slit into each chicken breast
half to form a pocket. Season the meat liberally inside and out with salt
and pepper. Place a few slices of the cheese, tomatoes, and 4 or 5 basil
leaves in each chicken breast. Wrap a piece of prosciutto around the center
of each chicken breast and use toothpicks to secure the prosciutto and
close the pockets, threading the toothpick parallel to the chicken breast so
it doesn't stick out and make browning difficult.

2 Select **SAUTÉ** and adjust to **MORE/HIGH** heat. When the pot is hot,
brush the chicken with the oil. Working in two batches, brown the
chicken breasts until golden brown on one side only, about 2 minutes.
Press **CANCEL**. Transfer the chicken to a plate.

3 Add the broth and vinegar to the pot. Place a trivet in the pot and
place the chicken breasts on the trivet; pour in any accumulated juices
from the plate. Lock on the lid, select the **PRESSURE COOK** function, and
adjust to **LOW** pressure for 8 minutes for 8-ounce chicken breasts and a
few minutes more if the chicken breasts are larger. Make sure the steam
valve is in the "Sealing" position and that the "Keep Warm" button is off.

4 When the cooking time is up, let the pressure come down naturally
for 5 minutes and then quick-release the remaining pressure. Make
sure the chicken is cooked through; an instant-read thermometer inserted
into the thickest part of the largest breast should register at least 160°F. If
the chicken isn't done, remove the trivet and set the chicken in the sauce.
Select **SAUTÉ**, adjust to **LESS/LOW** heat, cover with a pan lid, and simmer
for a few minutes until it is done. Transfer the chicken to a plate, remove
the toothpicks, and cover loosely with foil. Remove the trivet from the pot.

5 Select **SAUTÉ** and adjust to **NORMAL/MEDIUM** heat. In a small bowl,
stir the flour and butter together until smooth. Gradually whisk the flour
mixture into the cooking liquid, 1 teaspoon at a time. Simmer, whisking
frequently, until the sauce is thickened and bubbling, 3 minutes. Press **CANCEL**.
Spoon the sauce over the chicken and serve.

CHICKEN WITH CREAMY ARTICHOKE SAUCE

Serves 4   Active time: 35 minutes   Total time: 1 hour 15 minutes

Chicken and artichokes are a natural pairing, especially when combined in a lemony cream sauce. This recipe makes plenty of sauce, so it's great served on top of something to catch the goodness, like orzo or rice.

4 to 6 bone-in chicken thighs, skin removed

2 tablespoons olive oil

Salt and pepper

¼ cup diced pancetta, from a ½-inch-thick slab, or chopped thick-cut bacon

1 small yellow onion, halved lengthwise and thinly sliced through the root end (about 1 cup)

2 garlic cloves, thinly sliced

¼ cup dry vermouth or dry white wine

¾ cup Homemade Chicken Broth (page 198) or low-sodium store-bought broth

1 (12-ounce) bag frozen artichoke hearts, defrosted (do not use marinated artichokes)

2 teaspoons cornstarch

¼ cup heavy cream

2 tablespoons fresh lemon juice

2 tablespoons chopped fresh Italian parsley

1 Brush the chicken with 1 tablespoon of the oil and season generously with salt and pepper. Select **SAUTÉ** and adjust to **MORE/HIGH** heat. When the pot is hot, brown the thighs meaty-side down in batches until browned, 4 minutes. (Alternatively, broil the oiled and seasoned chicken thighs on a foil-lined baking until browned, 6 minutes.) Transfer to a plate.

2 Add the remaining 1 tablespoon oil to the pot. When the oil is hot, add the pancetta and onion. Cook, stirring frequently, until the onion is tender, 5 minutes. Add the vermouth and cook for 1 minute to burn off some of the alcohol. Press **CANCEL**.

3 Add the chicken, any accumulated juices from the plate, and the broth to the pot. Put the artichokes on top of the chicken, but do not stir them in. Lock on the lid, select the **PRESSURE COOK** function, and adjust to **HIGH** pressure for 10 minutes. Make sure the steam valve is in the "Sealing" position and that the "Keep Warm" button is off.

4 When the cooking time is up, let the pressure come down naturally for 10 minutes and then quick-release the remaining pressure. Use a slotted spoon to transfer the chicken and artichoke hearts to a serving platter and loosely tent with foil.

5 In a small bowl, mix the cornstarch with 1 tablespoon cold water until smooth. Add the mixture to the pot, select **SAUTÉ**, and adjust to **NORMAL/MEDIUM** heat. Cook, stirring occasionally, until the sauce is thick and bubbling, 2 minutes. Add the cream and lemon juice to the pot and stir to combine. Press **CANCEL**. Season with salt and pepper. Pour the sauce over the chicken and artichokes. Sprinkle with the parsley and serve.

CHICKEN CACCIATORE

Serves 4   Active time: 20 minutes   Total time: 50 minutes

Braising chicken legs with tomatoes and wild mushrooms in the Instant Pot yields fall-apart tender chicken and plenty of rich, woodsy sauce. Serve with Herbed Polenta (page 97) or fresh pappardelle pasta to catch all the saucy goodness.

1	ounce dried mixed wild mushrooms
1	tablespoon finely chopped fresh sage, or 1½ teaspoons dried
	Salt and pepper
4	bone-in chicken thighs, skin removed
1	tablespoon olive oil
4	bone-in chicken drumsticks, skin removed
1	medium yellow onion, halved lengthwise and thinly sliced through the root end
¼	cup diced pancetta, from a ½-inch-thick slab, or chopped thick-cut bacon
4	medium garlic cloves, finely chopped
¼	cup dry vermouth or dry white wine
1¼	cups crushed tomatoes
1	bay leaf
1	tablespoon cornstarch
¼	cup finely chopped fresh Italian parsley

1 In a microwave-safe measuring cup, combine 1 cup water with the dried mushrooms, and microwave on high heat for 1 minute to soften. (Alternatively, place the mushrooms in a small bowl and cover with 1 cup boiling water; set aside for 30 minutes while preparing the rest of the dish.)

2 Select **SAUTÉ** and adjust to **MORE/HIGH** heat. In a small bowl, mix the sage with 1 teaspoon salt and ½ teaspoon pepper. Brush the thighs with the oil and rub the sage mixture all over the chicken pieces. When the pot is hot, place the chicken thighs meaty-side down in the pot and cook until golden brown, 3 minutes. (Do not brown the drumsticks.) Transfer the chicken to a plate.

3 Add the onion and pancetta to the pot and cook, stirring occasionally, until the onion is tender and the pancetta fat has rendered, 4 minutes. Add the garlic and cook until fragrant, 45 seconds. Add the vermouth and cook for 1 minute to burn off some of the alcohol. Press **CANCEL**.

4 Chop the mushrooms and reserve the soaking liquid. Add the mushrooms and ½ cup of the reserved soaking liquid to the pot; save the remaining soaking liquid for another use or discard. Add the tomatoes and bay leaf and stir to combine. Place all the chicken pieces in the sauce, turning to coat. Lock on the lid, select the **PRESSURE COOK** function, and adjust to **HIGH** pressure for 12 minutes. Make sure the steam valve is in the "Sealing" position and that the "Keep Warm" button is off.

5 When the cooking time is up, let the pressure come down naturally for 10 minutes and then quick-release the remaining pressure. Transfer the chicken to a large serving bowl and cover loosely with foil.

6 In a small bowl, mix the cornstarch with 1 tablespoon cold water and stir until smooth. Select **SAUTÉ** and adjust to **NORMAL/MEDIUM** heat. Spoon off any clear liquid fat floating on top of the sauce, if desired, and discard. Add the cornstarch mixture to the pot and simmer until the sauce is bubbling, 2 minutes. Press **CANCEL**. Discard the bay leaf. Season the sauce with salt and pepper and pour it over the chicken. Serve garnished with the parsley.

🍲 CHICKEN PICCATA WITH SPAGHETTI

Serves 4   Active time: 20 minutes   Total time: 40 minutes

A trattoria favorite, *piccata* is a dish of thin veal or chicken cutlets browned in butter before being sautéed in a lemon-and-caper sauce. In this riff on the classic, I add spaghetti (it cooks perfectly in the same time as the chicken) and spinach or chard to sneak some veggies into this otherwise decadent dish. You'll need very small (6-ounce) chicken breasts for this recipe; if you have large (10- to 12-ounce) breast halves, split them in half horizontally.

3   tablespoons all-purpose flour

    Salt and pepper

4   small (6-ounce) boneless, skinless chicken breast halves (see Headnote)

2   tablespoons olive oil

1½ tablespoons unsalted butter

1   large shallot, thinly sliced

3   tablespoons drained capers

5   medium garlic cloves, thinly sliced

¼   cup dry vermouth or dry white wine

2¾ cups Homemade Chicken Broth (page 198) or low-sodium store-bought broth

8   ounces dry (uncooked) spaghetti, broken in half

2   cups loosely packed baby spinach or chopped chard leaves

1½ teaspoons finely grated lemon zest

2   tablespoons fresh lemon juice

1   On a dinner plate, combine the flour with ¾ teaspoon salt and ½ teaspoon pepper. Dredge the chicken in the flour and shake off any excess.

2   Put the oil and butter in the pot, select **SAUTÉ**, and adjust to **MORE/HIGH** heat. When the oil mixture is hot, brown the chicken in batches on one side only, about 4 minutes per batch. Transfer the chicken to a plate. Add the shallot, capers, and garlic to the pot and cook until fragrant, 1 minute. Add the vermouth and cook for 1 minute to burn off some of the alcohol. Press **CANCEL**.

3   Add the broth and pasta to the pot and stir to combine. Place the chicken and any accumulated juices on the plate in the pot on top of the pasta but do not stir them in. Lock on the lid, select the **PRESSURE COOK** function, and adjust to **LOW** pressure for 5 minutes. Make sure the steam valve is in the "Sealing" position and that the "Keep Warm" button is off.

4   When the cooking time is up, quick-release the pressure. Remove the lid and insert an instant-read thermometer into the center of the thickest part of one piece of chicken; it should register 160°F. If it's not done, cover the pot with a regular lid and let the mixture stand for a minute; the residual heat will finish cooking the chicken.

5   Transfer the chicken to plate. Add the spinach, lemon zest, and lemon juice to the pasta mixture and stir with tongs, breaking up any pasta clumps. Let the mixture sit in the appliance for 5 minutes for the sauce to thicken. Season with salt and pepper. Mound the pasta on four dinner plates and top with the chicken and sauce. Serve.

CHICKEN SALTIMBOCCA WITH CHEESY POTATOES

Serves 4 | Active time: 20 minutes | Total time: 45 minutes

This two-step, one-pot meal starts with braised boneless chicken thighs wrapped in prosciutto and sage, a dish called *saltimbocca*, or "jump in the mouth," in Italian. The cooking liquid is used to pressure-cook sliced potatoes for a quick 2-minute side dish that is then finished with melty Fontina cheese—think Italianized scalloped potatoes. Talk about a crowd-pleaser!

8   boneless, skinless chicken thighs, fat trimmed

4   slices prosciutto, halved lengthwise to make 8 strips

8   large fresh sage leaves

    Salt and pepper

2   tablespoons olive oil

1   tablespoon unsalted butter

4   medium garlic cloves, thinly sliced

¼   cup Marsala wine or dry sherry

¼   cup Homemade Chicken Broth (page 198) or low-sodium store-bought broth

1½   pounds Yukon Gold potatoes, peeled and cut crosswise into ¼-inch-thick slices

1   cup grated Fontina cheese (2 ounces)

1. Roll the edges of each chicken thigh in slightly to create a tidy package and wrap each one with a strip of prosciutto. Place a sage leaf on top of the prosciutto in the center of each chicken thigh and secure the leaf and the prosciutto to the chicken with a toothpick, threading the toothpick parallel to the chicken thigh so it doesn't stick out and make browning difficult. Season all over with salt and pepper.

2. Put the oil and butter in the pot, select **SAUTÉ**, and adjust to **MORE/HIGH** heat. When the oil mixture is hot, working in batches, add the chicken thighs, sage leaf–side down, and brown until golden brown on just one side, about 4 minutes per batch. Transfer to a plate and set aside.

3. Add the garlic to the pot and cook until fragrant, 45 seconds. Add the wine, scraping up any browned bits from the bottom of the pot, and simmer for 1 minute to burn off some of the alcohol. Press **CANCEL**.

4. Arrange the chicken thighs in the pot, sage leaf–side up, in an even layer. Add any accumulated juices from the plate to the pot along with the broth. Lock on the lid, select the **PRESSURE COOK** function, and adjust to **HIGH** pressure for 8 minutes. Make sure the steam valve is in the "Sealing" position and that the "Keep Warm" button is off.

5. When the cooking time is up, quick-release the pressure. Unlock the lid, transfer the chicken thighs to a serving plate, cover with foil, and set aside. Add the potatoes to the pot, season with salt and pepper, and stir to coat. Lock on the lid, select the **PRESSURE COOK** function, and adjust to **HIGH** pressure for 2 minutes. Make sure the steam valve is in the "Sealing" position and that the "Keep Warm" button is off.

6. When the cooking time is up, quick-release the pressure. Sprinkle the cheese over the potatoes, replace the lid slightly ajar, and let the mixture stand for a few minutes to melt the cheese. Stir to combine the cheese, potatoes, and liquid in the pot. Serve with the chicken.

CHICKEN PEPERONATA

Serves 4   Active time: 10 minutes   Total time: 40 minutes

I was introduced to sweet-sour *peperonata* while working in the kitchen at Trattoria Antica Torre in Barbaresco, Italy. I fell in love with the combination of sweet peppers, rosemary, and balsamic vinegar. There, the chef braised rabbit in the sauce for hours, but the same flavor combo works well with chicken and a quick stint in the Instant Pot, too. Serve with polenta or crusty bread to sop up the sauce.

4   small (8-ounce) boneless, skinless chicken breast halves

1   teaspoon granulated garlic

Salt and pepper

1   tablespoon olive oil

1   medium yellow onion, halved and sliced through the root end

1   red bell pepper, thinly sliced

1   yellow bell pepper, thinly sliced

2   teaspoons finely chopped fresh rosemary

1   cup tomato puree

1   tablespoon balsamic vinegar

1 Season the chicken all over with the granulated garlic, salt, and black pepper and set aside. Put the oil in the pot, select **SAUTÉ**, and adjust to **MORE/HIGH** heat. Add the onion, bell peppers, and rosemary and cook, stirring occasionally, until they are starting to become limp, 6 minutes. Press **CANCEL**.

2 Add the tomato puree and stir to combine. Place the chicken breasts on top of the bell pepper mixture. Lock on the lid, select the **PRESSURE COOK** function, and adjust to **LOW** pressure for 8 minutes for 8-ounce chicken breasts, or a minute more if they are larger. Make sure the steam valve is in the "Sealing" position and that the "Keep Warm" button is off.

3 When the cooking time is up, let the pressure come down naturally for 5 minutes and then quick-release the remaining pressure. Test the thickest part of the largest chicken breast with an instant-read thermometer; the chicken is done when the thermometer registers 160°F. If the chicken is done, transfer it to a large plate and tent it with foil. If the chicken is not done, leave it in the pot while simmering the sauce.

4 Stir the vinegar into the sauce, select **SAUTÉ**, adjust to **MORE/HIGH** heat, and simmer for 4 minutes to meld the flavors and thicken the sauce a bit. Press **CANCEL**. Season the sauce with salt and black pepper. Serve the chicken with the sauce spooned over the top.

DUCK RAGÙ

Makes 6 cups; serves 8 | Active time: 25 minutes | Total time: 1 hour 30 minutes

Venice is set in a lagoon, so it's fitting that they've got a million delicious ways to cook duck. The inclusion of cinnamon and cloves in savory dishes like this is a reminder that Venice was built on the riches gained from the spice trade with the East. The Instant Pot breaks down duck legs quickly into a meltingly tender, rich meat sauce. Serve with thick ribbons of pappardelle pasta, paccheri (large rigatoni), or potato gnocchi.

2   duck legs with skin (1½ to 1¾ pounds total)

1   tablespoon olive oil

    Salt and pepper

1   large yellow onion, finely chopped

1   large carrot, finely chopped

1   celery rib, finely chopped

2   teaspoons finely chopped fresh rosemary

½   teaspoon baking soda

2   tablespoons tomato paste

3   medium garlic cloves, finely chopped

½   cup dry red wine

1   (28-ounce) can whole peeled San Marzano tomatoes, chopped (see Note, page 192), with their juices

½   cinnamon stick

4   whole cloves

1   bay leaf

1   Select **SAUTÉ** and adjust to **MORE/HIGH** heat. When the pot is hot, brush the duck legs with the oil and season them liberally with salt and pepper. Place the duck in the pot and cook until well browned, 5 minutes per side. Transfer the duck to a plate and discard all but 1 tablespoon of the fat.

2   Add the onion, carrot, celery, rosemary, and baking soda and cook until the vegetables are tender, 4 minutes. Add the tomato paste and garlic and cook, stirring frequently, until the garlic is fragrant, 1 minute. Add the wine and cook for 1 minute to burn off some of the alcohol. Press **CANCEL**.

3   Add the tomatoes, cinnamon, cloves, and bay leaf and stir to combine. Add the duck legs and push them down to submerge them in the sauce. Lock on the lid, select the **PRESSURE COOK** function, and adjust to **HIGH** pressure for 30 minutes. Make sure the steam valve is in the "Sealing" position and that the "Keep Warm" button is off.

4   When cooking time is up, let the pressure come down naturally for 10 minutes and then quick-release the remaining pressure. Transfer the duck legs to a cutting board. Discard the skin and bones, coarsely chop the meat, and return it to the pot. Fish out the cinnamon stick, bay leaves, and cloves (if you can find them) and discard.

5   Select **SAUTÉ** and adjust to **NORMAL/MEDIUM** heat. When the liquid comes to a simmer, liquid fat will pool on the top around the edges of the pot. Spoon off the fat and discard. Press **CANCEL**. Season with salt and pepper.

The cooled sauce can be stored in an airtight container in the refrigerator for up to 3 days or in the freezer for up to 3 months. Defrost in the refrigerator overnight if frozen before reheating gently.

TURKEY BREAST WITH CHESTNUT STUFFING

Serves 4 to 6 | Active time: 25 minutes | Total time: 1 hour 30 minutes

This is a great alternative to roasting a whole bird at Thanksgiving. It's just as impressive, but quick to prepare. The stuffing is classically Italian in that it's more meat than bread and includes chestnuts, a seasonal treat.

2 slices sandwich bread (3 ounces), torn in pieces

2⅓ cups Homemade Chicken Broth (page 198) or low-sodium store-bought broth

⅔ cup (3½ ounces) roasted peeled chestnuts, chopped

¾ cup ground dark meat turkey or veal (6 ounces)

2 tablespoons finely chopped fresh Italian parsley

2 teaspoons finely chopped fresh rosemary

Salt and pepper

1 (2½-pound) boneless, skin-on turkey breast half

Olive oil, for brushing

1 small yellow onion, quartered

2 celery ribs, coarsely chopped

1 medium carrot, chopped

2 tablespoons unsalted butter

2 tablespoons all-purpose flour

Soy sauce, for color (optional)

1 Place the bread in a large bowl and sprinkle with ⅓ cup of the broth; let stand for 5 minutes to soften. Add the chestnuts, ground meat, parsley, rosemary, ¾ teaspoon salt, and a few grinds of pepper. Stir until well combined. Set aside.

2 Place the turkey breast skin-side up on a large cutting board. Holding a boning knife parallel to the cutting board, slice the breast lengthwise in half but do not cut all the way through, stopping 1 inch before cutting through the meat entirely at the opposite edge. Open out the meat as you would a book so that it lies flat. The skin should be on the bottom and the meat will look roughly like a rectangle.

3 Cover the meat with plastic wrap and pound with the smooth side of a meat mallet until the meat is ½ to ¾ inch thick. (Don't worry if there are a few tears.) Remove the plastic and season the meat with salt and pepper. Spread the stuffing over the turkey breast, leaving a 1-inch border around the edges. Starting on the long side, roll the meat up, tucking in the ends and any escaped stuffing, if necessary. Place the turkey roll seam-side down on a cutting board. Tie with butcher's twine at 2-inch intervals to hold the roast together. Brush with olive oil and season with salt and pepper.

4 Select **SAUTÉ** and adjust to **MORE/HIGH** heat. When the pot is hot, add the turkey, seam-side up, and cook until browned, 3 minutes. Press **CANCEL**. Transfer the turkey to a plate. Place a trivet with handles in the pot. Add the remaining 2 cups broth, the onion, celery, and carrot to the pot. Place the turkey on the trivet. Lock on the lid, select the **PRESSURE COOK** function, and adjust to **HIGH** pressure for 30 minutes. Make sure the steam valve is in the "Sealing" position and that the "Keep Warm" button is off.

5 When the cooking time is up, let the pressure come down naturally, about 10 minutes, and then quick-release the remaining pressure. An instant-read thermometer inserted into the center of the turkey roll should register 160°F. If it doesn't, cover the pot with a regular pot lid, select **SAUTÉ**, adjust to **LESS/LOW** heat, and simmer briefly until 160°F is reached.

6 Transfer the turkey to a cutting board and cover loosely with foil. Strain the broth into a large glass measuring cup and spoon off the fat floating on the top. Alternatively, pour the broth into a gravy separator and discard the fat.

7 Add the butter to the pot, select **SAUTÉ**, and adjust to **MORE/HIGH** heat. Whisk in the flour and cook for 1 minute. Whisk in the strained broth and cook until bubbling, 3 minutes. Press **CANCEL**. Season the gravy with salt, pepper, and a little soy sauce for color, if desired.

8 Slice the turkey roast crosswise into ½-inch-thick slices, discarding the butcher's twine. Serve with the gravy.

TURKEY-STUFFED BELL PEPPERS

This old-school favorite is made lighter by using lean Italian turkey sausage instead of pork. The raw meat cooks directly in the peppers in the Instant Pot—there's no need to brown it first. I've included instructions for making rice with chicken broth for added flavor, but you can use plain cooked leftover rice, quinoa, or farro as a shortcut; you will need 2 cups cooked grains for this recipe.

1 cup long-grain rice

1½ cups Homemade Chicken Broth (page 198) or low-sodium store-bought broth

2 teaspoons olive oil

Salt and pepper

4 medium bell peppers, top ½ inch of stem end removed, seeds discarded

12 ounces bulk Italian turkey or chicken sausage

1 cup canned tomato sauce

1 teaspoon dried Italian seasoning

1 teaspoon granulated garlic

½ cup grated Parmesan cheese

½ cup fresh basil leaves, torn

1 Place the rice in a fine-mesh sieve and rinse well. Place the rice, 1 cup of the broth, the oil, ½ teaspoon salt, and a few grinds of black pepper in the pot. Lock on the lid and select the **RICE** function, or select the **PRESSURE COOK** function and adjust to **HIGH** pressure for 8 minutes. Make sure the steam valve is in the "Sealing" position and that the "Keep Warm" button is off. When the cooking time is up, let the pressure come down naturally for 10 minutes and then quick-release the remaining pressure.

2 Transfer the rice to a large bowl. Add the raw sausage and mix well to combine. Spoon the rice and sausage mixture into the peppers.

3 Rinse out the pot and return it to the appliance. In a small bowl, combine the remaining ½ cup broth with the tomato sauce, Italian seasoning, garlic, and a few grinds of black pepper. Pour about three-quarters of the tomato sauce mixture into the base of the pot. Place a trivet with handles in the pot and set the peppers on top of the trivet. Spoon the remaining sauce over the peppers and sprinkle with the cheese.

4 Lock on the lid, select the **PRESSURE COOK** function, and adjust to **HIGH** pressure for 15 minutes. Make sure the steam valve is in the "Sealing" position and that the "Keep Warm" button is off.

5 When the cooking time is up, let the pressure come down naturally for 10 minutes and then quick-release the remaining pressure. Remove the trivet from the pot and transfer the peppers to dinner plates. Spoon the sauce over the peppers and sprinkle with the basil.

TURKEY BREAST WITH TONNATO

This classic dish of poached turkey with *tonnato*, a creamy tuna-mayonnaise sauce, is from the Piedmont region of Italy. The dish is traditionally made with slow-poached veal breast, but boneless turkey breast is lovely and is easier to find. Pair the turkey with a green salad for a light entrée, or serve by itself as a first course or buffet item. The leftover turkey and sauce make great sandwiches the next day.

1   medium yellow onion, chopped

1   large carrot, chopped

1   celery rib, chopped

3   sprigs fresh thyme

1   bay leaf

1   (2-pound) boneless, skin-on turkey breast half

Salt and pepper

1   (5-ounce) can tuna packed in oil, drained

¾   cup olive oil mayonnaise or regular mayonnaise

2½ tablespoons fresh lemon juice

1½ tablespoons capers

¼   cup finely chopped fresh Italian parsley

1 Place the onion, carrot, celery, thyme, bay leaf, and 2 cups cold water in the pot. Season the turkey breast all over with salt and place it skin-side up on top of the vegetables. Lock on the lid, select the **PRESSURE COOK** function, and adjust to **HIGH** pressure for 12 minutes. Make sure the steam valve is in the "Sealing" position and that the "Keep Warm" button is off.

2 When the cooking time is up, let the pressure come down naturally for 10 minutes and then quick-release the remaining pressure. Insert an instant-read thermometer into the thickest part of the turkey breast; the meat is done when the thermometer reaches 160°F. If the meat is not done, turn the breast over, cover with a regular pot lid, select **SAUTÉ**, adjust to **NORMAL/MEDIUM** heat, and simmer until done.

3 Remove the turkey breast from the pot, place on a plate, and let rest at room temperature for 10 minutes. Transfer to the refrigerator and chill until cooled to room temperature, about 1 hour. Strain the broth and reserve it for another use.

4 While the turkey cools, make the *tonnato* sauce: In a food processor or blender, blend the tuna, mayonnaise, lemon juice, and 2 teaspoons of the capers until smooth. Season with salt and pepper.

5 Discard the turkey skin. Slice the meat with a sharp carving knife into very thin slices and arrange on a large serving platter. Spoon some of the sauce over the top and sprinkle with the parsley and remaining capers.

The turkey can be wrapped in foil and the sauce stored in an airtight container; they will keep in the refrigerator for up to 3 days.

PORK, BEEF, AND LAMB

Italian cuisine is full of delicious, long-braised meat dishes that are designed to bubble away for hours on the back burner. Cooking these recipes under pressure in the Instant Pot yields dishes with just as much flavor and tenderness much more quickly.

To help build a flavorful sauce, most of these meaty recipes brown the meat before the liquid is added. Since the bottom of the Instant Pot is slightly convex, oil tends to spread to the edges of the pot, leaving the center dry—which can cause the meat you are searing to stick. For perfect searing, heat the pot on SAUTÉ, MORE/HIGH until the screen reads HOT. Brush the meat with a small amount of oil and season it, then add it to the pot. For recipes with lots of little pieces of meat, like cubed lamb, that would require browning in the pot in batches, browning under the broiler is a good time-saving alternative, and I include instructions for both options.

Once the meat is done cooking, it's best to let the pressure come down naturally for at least 10 minutes. This gradual reduction of pressure allows the meat fibers to relax slowly and redistribute moisture throughout, similar to when you let a roast rest before carving it. The intense environment created by quick-releasing the pressure, on the other hand, tends to break apart the meat fibers, leaving your roasts a bit frayed. Your patience with the slow-release method will be rewarded with juicy roasts, tender meatballs, and fork-tender lamb in the following recipes.

BRAISED PORK LOIN WITH MILK AND SAGE

Serves 4 to 6   **Active time: 20 minutes**   **Total time: 1 hour 10 minutes**

In Tuscany, cooks braise pork loins in milk to tenderize the meat and create a delicious sauce that caramelizes to a beautiful gravy in the bottom of the pot. The Instant Pot reduces the cooking time (and cleanup) by about half. The sauce looks a little curdled at first, but don't panic—it's an authentic aspect of the dish, and when you whisk in the flour and butter at the end, the sauce thickens and the milk proteins will disperse.
Serve the roast with mashed potatoes or soft polenta.

1 **(2¼ to 2½-pound) well-marbled pork loin roast**

2 **tablespoons olive oil**

Salt and pepper

1 **medium yellow onion, halved lengthwise and sliced through the root end**

1 **tablespoon chopped fresh sage leaves, or 1½ teaspoons dried**

1 **teaspoon chopped fresh rosemary**

½ **cup Homemade Chicken Broth (page 198) or low-sodium store-bought broth**

1 **cup 2% milk**

3 **garlic cloves, thinly sliced**

2 **tablespoons unsalted butter, at room temperature**

2 **tablespoons all-purpose flour**

1 Select **SAUTÉ** and adjust to **MORE/HIGH** heat. Brush the pork with 1 tablespoon of the oil and generously season it all over with salt and pepper. When the pot is hot, add the pork and cook until browned on all sides, about 6 minutes. Transfer to a plate.

2 Add the remaining 1 tablespoon oil to the pot, the onion, sage, and rosemary and cook, stirring occasionally and scraping up any browned bits on the bottom, until the onion is beginning to brown, 5 minutes. Add the broth and cook, stirring frequently, for 1 minute. Press **CANCEL**.

3 Add the milk and garlic and stir to combine. Return the pork to the pot, turn the pork in the milk mixture to coat, and then place it fatty-side up. Lock on the lid, select the **PRESSURE COOK** function, and adjust to **HIGH** pressure for 20 minutes for a 2¼-pound roast or 22 minutes for a 2½-pound roast. Make sure the steam valve is in the "Sealing" position and that the "Keep Warm" button is off.

4 When the cooking time is up, let the pressure come down naturally for 10 minutes and then quick-release the remaining pressure. Check the roast with an instant-read thermometer; it should register at least 135°F. If the roast needs more time, cover the pot with a regular lid, select **SAUTÉ**, and adjust to **MORE/HIGH** for 5 minutes. Check the roast again and transfer it to a serving platter when it is done. Tent with foil.

5 In a small bowl, combine the butter and flour and stir until smooth. Select **SAUTÉ** and adjust to **NORMAL/MEDIUM** heat. Gradually whisk the flour mixture into the cooking liquid and simmer, whisking frequently, until thickened, 3 minutes. Press **CANCEL**. Slice the roast crosswise into thin slices and serve with the sauce.

BRAISED PORK CHOPS WITH FIGS AND BALSAMIC VINEGAR

Serves 4   Active time: 15 minutes   Total time: 45 minutes

This sweet-and-sour braised pork chop recipe features fresh figs, but you can also make it with dried figs if fresh aren't in season. Look for meaty, ¾-inch-thick, center-cut pork chops; they have the most marbling and are tender and moist when braised.

4   (6- to 8-ounce) center-cut bone-in pork chops

2   tablespoons olive oil

Salt and pepper

1   large yellow onion, halved lengthwise and sliced through the root end

2   teaspoons finely chopped fresh rosemary

2   medium garlic cloves, finely chopped

2   tablespoons balsamic vinegar

1   cup Homemade Chicken Broth (page 198) or low-sodium store-bought broth

1   pint fresh figs (12 ounces), quartered, or 8 dried figs, halved

1   tablespoon unsalted butter, at room temperature

1   tablespoon all-purpose flour

1 Using a paring knife, cut two slits in the fat around the edges of each chop but do not cut into the meat itself; this will prevent the chops from curling up as they cook. Select **SAUTÉ** and adjust to **MORE/HIGH** heat. When the pot is hot, brush the chops with 1 tablespoon of the oil and season liberally with salt and pepper. Sear the chops in batches until browned, about 3 minutes per side. (Alternatively, broil the pork chops on a foil-lined baking sheet on a rack set 3 inches below the broiling element until browned, 3 minutes per side.) Transfer the chops to a plate.

2 Add the remaining 1 tablespoon oil to the pot. Add the onion and rosemary and cook until tender, 4 minutes. Add the garlic and cook until fragrant, 45 seconds. Add the vinegar and simmer for 30 seconds, scraping up any browned bits from the bottom of the pot. Press **CANCEL**.

3 Add the chops, any accumulated juices on the plate, and the broth to the pot. (The pork chops don't need to be in a single layer.) Nestle the figs in among the chops; if using dried figs, submerge them in the broth. Lock on the lid, select the **PRESSURE COOK** function, and adjust to **HIGH** pressure for 10 minutes. Make sure the steam valve is in the "Sealing" position and that the "Keep Warm" button is off.

4 When the cooking time is up, let the pressure come down naturally for 10 minutes. Quick-release any remaining pressure. Transfer the chops and figs to a serving platter and cover loosely with foil.

5 In a small bowl, combine the butter and flour and stir until smooth. Select **SAUTÉ** and adjust to **NORMAL/MEDIUM** heat. Gradually whisk the flour mixture into the cooking liquid and simmer until the sauce is thickened and bubbling, 3 minutes. Press **CANCEL**. Pour the sauce over the chops and serve.

🍲 PORK ROAST WITH WILD MUSHROOMS AND POTATOES

Serves 4 to 6 | Active time: 25 minutes | Total time: 2 hours

The richness of pork shoulder and mushrooms is countered here by the slightly resinous flavor of dried juniper berries, a common addition in Northern Italian regions like Friuli. Adding potatoes during the last 30 minutes of cooking makes this a one-pot meal, but they are optional.

1   (2½- to 3-pound) pork shoulder roast, tied

2   tablespoons olive oil

12   dried juniper berries, coarsely crushed in a mortar and pestle

Salt and pepper

1   medium yellow onion, halved lengthwise and sliced through the root end

1   teaspoon dried marjoram or thyme

½   cup dry vermouth or dry white wine

½   cup Homemade Chicken or Beef Broth (page 198 or 199) or low-sodium store-bought broth

1   ounce dried porcini mushrooms (about 1 cup)

1   bay leaf

1½   pounds baby Yukon Gold potatoes (about the size of a golf ball or smaller)

1   tablespoon cornstarch

1 Select **SAUTÉ** and adjust to **MORE/HIGH** heat. When the pot is hot, brush the roast with 1 tablespoon of the oil. Rub the juniper and 1 teaspoon each of salt and pepper into the meat. Sear the roast until browned all over, about 10 minutes. Transfer to a plate.

2 Add the remaining 1 tablespoon oil to the pot. Add the onion and marjoram and cook until the onion is tender, 4 minutes. Add the vermouth and simmer for 1 minute to boil off some of the alcohol. Press **CANCEL**.

3 Add the broth, mushrooms, and bay leaf. Transfer the pork and any accumulated juices on the plate to the pot. Lock on the lid, select the **PRESSURE COOK** function, and adjust to **HIGH** pressure for 1 hour. Make sure the steam valve is in the "Sealing" position and that the "Keep Warm" button is off.

4 When the cooking time is up, quick-release the pressure. Add the potatoes to the pot. Lock on the lid, select the **PRESSURE COOK** function, and adjust to **HIGH** pressure for 30 minutes. Make sure the steam valve is in the "Sealing" position and that the "Keep Warm" button is off.

5 When the cooking time is up, let the pressure come down naturally, about 15 minutes. Transfer the roast to a cutting board and the potatoes to a bowl. Loosely cover with foil.

6 Select **SAUTÉ** and adjust to **NORMAL/MEDIUM** heat. When the liquid comes to a simmer, liquid fat will pool on the top around the edges of the pot. Spoon off the fat and discard it.

7 Mix the cornstarch with 1 tablespoon water, add it to the pot, and simmer until thickened and bubbling, 1 minute. Press **CANCEL**. Slice the pork into thin slices and serve with the sauce.

The roast and sauce can be stored in separate airtight containers in the refrigerator for up to 5 days. Reheat gently before serving.

ITALIAN SAUSAGE AND PEPPER BOMBER SANDWICHES

Serves 4   Active time: 10 minutes   Total time: 35 minutes

This quick, family-pleasing recipe is something like an Italianified version of French dip sandwiches—hoagies piled high with braised sausages, peppers, and onions served with the tomato-and-herb braising liquid for dipping. For a leaner sandwich, choose turkey or chicken sausages.

1 tablespoon olive oil

4 sweet or spicy Italian sausage links

1 medium yellow onion, halved lengthwise and sliced through the root end

1 red bell pepper, sliced

1 green bell pepper, sliced

¾ cup crushed tomatoes

¼ cup Homemade Chicken or Beef Broth (page 198 or 199) or low-sodium store-bought broth

1 teaspoon fennel seeds

1 teaspoon dried Italian seasoning

4 crusty sandwich rolls, split lengthwise and toasted

1 Put the oil in the pot, select **SAUTÉ**, and adjust to **MORE/HIGH** heat. When the oil is hot, add the sausages and cook until browned, about 3 minutes per side. Transfer the sausages to a plate. Add the onion and bell peppers to the pot and cook, stirring occasionally, until the vegetables are beginning to soften, 5 minutes. Press **CANCEL**.

2 Add the tomatoes, broth, fennel seeds, and Italian seasoning and stir to combine. Nestle the sausages into the bell pepper mixture. Lock on the lid, select the **PRESSURE COOK** function, and adjust to **HIGH** pressure for 4 minutes. Make sure the steam valve is in the "Sealing" position and that the "Keep Warm" button is off.

3 When the cooking time is up, let the pressure come down naturally for 10 minutes and then quick-release the remaining pressure. Place the sausages and vegetables on the buns. Pour the cooking sauce into ramekins and serve on the side for dipping.

PORK LOIN ALLA PORCHETTA

Serves 4 to 6 | Active time: 20 | Total time: 1 hour 30 minutes

Porchetta is made by boning a whole pig, stuffing it with herbs, and roasting it on a spit . . . not exactly an undertaking for home cooks. Instead, I love to butterfly a pork loin, stuff it with herby ground pork stuffing, and braise it in the Instant Pot. Same moist, porky goodness, lots less time. I've included instructions on how to butterfly the roast, but you could ask your butcher to do it for you, if you like.

12	ounces ground pork
¼	cup grated Parmesan cheese
4	medium garlic cloves, finely chopped
1	tablespoon finely chopped fresh rosemary, plus 2 sprigs
2	teaspoons finely chopped fresh sage, or 1 teaspoon dried
¾	teaspoon fennel seeds, crushed
¼	teaspoon red chile flakes
	Salt and pepper
1	(2-pound) center-cut pork loin roast
	Olive oil, for brushing
¾	cup Homemade Chicken Broth (page 198) or low-sodium store-bought broth
2	tablespoons unsalted butter, at room temperature
2	tablespoons all-purpose flour

1 In a large bowl, combine the ground pork, cheese, garlic, chopped rosemary, sage, fennel, red chile flakes, 1 teaspoon salt, and several grinds of black pepper and stir well to combine.

2 Place the pork loin on a cutting board with the fatty side up and the short end facing you. Holding a sharp boning knife parallel to the cutting board, slice lengthwise down the roast about 1 inch from the top of the roast, but do not cut all the way through to the other side, leaving a ½-inch "hinge" on side of the roast. Flip the top flap of meat open as if turning the page of a book.

3 Just next to the hinge where the "page" opens, make a ½-inch cut straight down into the meat (be sure not to cut all the way through to the bottom of the roast). Turn the knife blade parallel to the cutting board and cut a second flap, working in the opposite direction as the first, again stopping before you cut all the way through, about ½ inch from the edge. Open the second flap; you will have a flat rectangle of meat.

4 Sprinkle the meat with salt and black pepper. Spread the ground pork mixture evenly over the meat, leaving a ¼-inch border all around. Starting on the short side (the side without the fatty top), roll the meat up into a cylinder, as you would a sleeping bag. Place the rolled roast fat side up, seam-side down on the cutting board and tie with butcher's string at 2-inch intervals.

5 Select **SAUTÉ** and adjust to **MORE/HIGH** heat. Brush the roast with the oil and season all over with salt and black pepper. When the pot is hot, add the roast and cook until browned on all sides, about 8 minutes. Press **CANCEL**. Place the roast fat-side up in the pot and add the broth and

(recipe continues)

(*continued from page 131*)

rosemary sprigs. Lock on the lid, select the **PRESSURE COOK** function, and adjust to **HIGH** pressure for 40 minutes. Make sure the steam valve is in the "Sealing" position and that the "Keep Warm" button is off.

6 When the cooking time is up, let the pressure come down naturally for 15 minutes and then quick-release the remaining pressure. Check the roast with an instant-read thermometer; it should register at least 135°F. If the roast needs more time, select **SAUTÉ**, adjust to **NORMAL/MEDIUM** heat, cover with a regular pan lid, and simmer until the roast reaches the correct temperature. Transfer the roast to a serving platter and tent with foil. Discard the rosemary sprigs.

7 In a small bowl, stir the butter and flour together until smooth. Select **SAUTÉ** and adjust to **NORMAL/MEDIUM** heat. Gradually whisk the flour mixture into the cooking liquid and simmer, whisking frequently, until thickened and bubbling, 3 minutes. Press **CANCEL**. Slice the roast crosswise into slices and discard the butcher's twine. Serve with the sauce.

MEATBALLS MARINARA

Serves 4   Active time: 20 minutes   Total time: 50 minutes

These tender meatballs conceal a big surprise—gooey melted mozzarella cheese centers! Broiling the meatballs for just 5 minutes gives them a nice browned appearance without the time-consuming process of browning them in the pot. This helps build a beefier sauce, but you can skip it and plop the raw meatballs right into the sauce in the pot if you'd like. Serve the meatballs and sauce with spaghetti or try them over polenta.

½   cup dry Italian-style bread crumbs

¼   cup heavy cream or half-and-half

1   egg yolk

8   ounces 80% lean ground chuck

8   ounces bulk sweet Italian pork sausage

¼   cup finely grated Parmesan cheese

1   teaspoon granulated garlic

½   teaspoon dried Italian seasoning

Salt and pepper

2   sticks mozzarella string cheese or about 2 ounces part-skim mozzarella, cut into ½-inch cubes

2   tablespoons olive oil

1   medium yellow onion, chopped

4   medium garlic cloves, finely chopped

½   cup dry red wine

1   (28-ounce) can crushed tomatoes

¼   cup chopped fresh basil leaves (optional)

1 Preheat the broiler and adjust an oven rack so it is 6 inches below the broiler element. Line a baking sheet with foil and spray it with cooking spray.

2 In a large bowl, combine the bread crumbs, cream, and egg yolk and stir to moisten the crumbs. Add the ground beef, sausage, Parmesan, granulated garlic, Italian seasoning, ¾ teaspoon salt, and several grinds of pepper and mix with your hands or a wooden spoon until well combined.

3 Divide the mixture into 16 portions, about 2 tablespoons each. Push a cube of cheese into the center of each portion of meat and then roll into spheres, making sure to cover the cheese completely. Set the meatballs on the prepared baking sheet and broil until browned on top, 5 minutes.

4 While the meatballs are broiling, make the sauce. Put the oil in the pot, select **SAUTÉ**, and adjust to **NORMAL/MEDIUM** heat. When the oil is hot, add the onion and cook, stirring frequently, until tender, 4 minutes. Add the garlic and cook until fragrant, 45 seconds. Add the wine and cook for 1 minute to burn off some of the alcohol. Add the tomatoes. Add ½ cup cold water to the tomato can, swish it around, and add it to pot. Press **CANCEL**.

5 Add the meatballs to the pot but don't stir. Lock on the lid, select the **PRESSURE COOK** function, and adjust to **HIGH** pressure for 5 minutes. Make sure the steam valve is in the "Sealing" position and that the "Keep Warm" button is off.

6 When the cooking time is up, let the pressure come down naturally for 10 minutes and then quick-release the remaining pressure. Serve the meatballs in the sauce, sprinkled with the basil.

The meatballs and sauce can be stored in an airtight container in the refrigerator for up to 5 days. Reheat gently before serving.

BAROLO-BRAISED BEEF ROAST

Serves 6 **Active time: 20 minutes** **Total time: 2 hours**

Barolo is a lush, tannic red wine made from Nebbiolo grapes in the Piedmont region of northwestern Italy. Though it's considered one of the best wines in Italy, there are bargains to be had, so you don't have to shed too many tears as you pour a cup into this meaty braise. If you can't find a reasonably priced Barolo, substitute another dry Italian red wine, like Dolcetto or Barbera. This pot roast is rustic and very tender; there will be some rough edges that fall off while slicing. For the neatest appearance, buy a cross-rib roast, which will have a more compact shape and slice more cleanly than flat chuck roasts. Serve with Herbed Polenta (page 97) or Truffled Celery Root Mashers (page 165).

1 (2½- to 3-pound) cross-rib chuck roast

2 tablespoons olive oil

Salt and pepper

1 medium yellow onion, finely chopped

1 large carrot, chopped

1 celery rib, chopped

1 teaspoon finely chopped fresh rosemary

½ teaspoon baking soda

3 medium garlic cloves, chopped

1 cup Barolo wine

½ cup boxed or canned diced tomatoes in puree

2 tablespoons unsalted butter, at room temperature

2 tablespoons all-purpose flour

1. Select **SAUTÉ** and adjust to **MORE/HIGH** heat. Brush the roast with 1 tablespoon of the oil and season liberally with salt and pepper. When the pot is hot, add the roast and cook until browned all over, 10 minutes. Transfer to a plate.

2. Add the remaining 1 tablespoon oil to the pot. Add the onion, carrot, celery, rosemary, and baking soda and cook until the vegetables are tender, 4 minutes. Add the garlic and cook until fragrant, 45 seconds. Add the wine and simmer for 1 minute to boil off some of the alcohol. Press **CANCEL**.

3. Add the tomatoes and stir to combine. Return the roast to the pot along with any accumulated juices on the plate. Lock on the lid, select the **PRESSURE COOK** function, and adjust to **HIGH** for 1½ hours. Make sure the steam valve is in the "Sealing" position and that the "Keep Warm" button is off.

4. When the cooking time is up, let the pressure come down naturally for 15 minutes and then quick-release the remaining pressure. Transfer the roast to a cutting board and loosely cover with foil. Select **SAUTÉ** and adjust to **NORMAL/MEDIUM** heat. When the liquid comes to a simmer, liquid fat will pool on the top around the edges of the pot. Spoon off the fat and discard.

5. In a small bowl, combine the butter and flour and stir until smooth. Gradually whisk the flour mixture into the cooking liquid. Simmer, whisking frequently, until the sauce is thickened and bubbling, 5 minutes. Press **CANCEL**. Season the sauce with salt and pepper.

6. Slice the beef and arrange it on a serving platter. Spoon the sauce over the meat.

The meat and sauce can be stored in an airtight container in the refrigerator for up to 5 days. Reheat gently before serving.

BEEF BRACIOLE

Serves 6 to 8   Active time: 30 minutes   Total time: 1 hour 20 minutes

This Sicilian dish of little beef rolls stuffed with herby bread crumbs and Italian cold cuts normally takes hours of simmering on the stovetop. This streamlined version is fork-tender in 25 minutes and is every bit as rib-sticking tasty. You can save time by purchasing thinly sliced beef scallopine from your butcher instead of pounding out the meat yourself. Serve this dish with short pasta like ziti.

2   cups fresh bread crumbs (from 3 slices sturdy white sandwich bread)

½   cup finely grated Pecorino Romano cheese

2   tablespoons chopped fresh Italian parsley

2   tablespoons chopped fresh basil

1   large egg

1   medium garlic clove, minced and smashed with the side of a knife into a paste

    Salt and pepper

2½ pounds eye of round or top round beef roast, or beef scallopine about ¼ inch thick

3   ounces thinly sliced prosciutto

3   ounces thinly sliced mortadella

2   tablespoons olive oil

½   cup dry red wine

3   cups Homemade Marinara (page 192) or jarred marinara sauce

1 In a medium bowl, combine the bread crumbs, cheese, parsley, basil, egg, garlic, ¼ teaspoon salt, and several grinds of pepper and stir to combine; set aside.

2 If making your own scallopine, slice the beef roast into ½-inch-thick slices. Place a slice of beef between two sheets of plastic wrap and pound with the flat side of a meat mallet until it is about ¼ inch thick. Repeat with the remaining slices.

3 Season the scallopine generously with salt and pepper. Place slices of the prosciutto and mortadella on the beef, tearing the cold cuts so they just cover the beef but don't creep out over the edges. Place about 2 tablespoons of the bread crumb mixture in the center of each piece of beef. Roll up the meat and secure the seams with toothpicks, threading the toothpicks parallel to the meat so they don't poke out too much and make browning the meat difficult. Push any of the filling that creeps out back into the center of the rolls.

4 Select **SAUTÉ** and adjust to **MORE/HIGH** heat. Brush the rolls with 1 tablespoon of the oil. When the pot is hot, add about 5 of the beef rolls and cook, turning them occasionally, until browned all over, 4 minutes. Place the rolls on a platter and repeat with the remaining rolls. With the pot empty, add the wine and cook, scraping up any browned bits from the bottom, until some of the alcohol burns off, 1 minute. Press **CANCEL**.

5 Add the marinara sauce and stir to combine. Place the rolls back in the pot and turn them with tongs to coat them in the sauce. Lock on the lid, select the **PRESSURE COOK** function, and adjust to **HIGH** pressure for 25 minutes. Make sure the steam valve is in the "Sealing" position and that the "Keep Warm" button is off.

(recipe continues)

(*continued from page 136*)

6 When the cooking time is up, let the pressure come down naturally for 15 minutes and then quick-release the remaining pressure. Transfer the beef rolls to a platter (you can remove the toothpicks now if you like, or leave them in). Cover loosely with foil.

7 Select **SAUTÉ**, adjust to **MORE/HIGH** heat, and simmer the sauce, uncovered, stirring frequently, until it has reduced slightly, 5 minutes. Using a ladle, spoon off any liquid fat floating on top of the sauce and discard it. Press **CANCEL**. Season the sauce with salt and pepper.

8 Pour the sauce over the beef rolls and serve.

The rolls and sauce can be stored in an airtight container in the refrigerator for up to 5 days. Reheat gently before serving.

OSSO BUCO

These veal shanks become so tender in the Instant Pot that you have to tie them around their circumference so they don't fall apart while cooking. In Milan, where this dish is from, the shanks are always served on saffron risotto, though their tender texture and velvety sauce are a good match for orzo or polenta, too.

4   (6- to 7-ounce) cross-cut veal shanks, about 1½ inches thick

2   tablespoons olive oil

Salt and pepper

1   medium yellow onion, finely chopped

1   medium carrot, finely chopped

1   celery rib, finely chopped

2   teaspoons chopped fresh thyme, or ½ teaspoon dried

½   teaspoon baking soda

1   medium garlic clove, finely chopped

2   tablespoons tomato paste

¼   cup dry vermouth or dry white wine

1½   cups Homemade Beef Broth (page 199) or low-sodium store-bought broth

½   cup crushed tomatoes

2   tablespoons unsalted butter, at room temperature

3   tablespoons all-purpose flour

1   Tie the veal shanks tightly around their circumference with butcher's twine to help hold them together while they cook. Select **SAUTÉ** and adjust to **MORE/HIGH** heat. Brush the shanks all over with 1 tablespoon of the oil and season generously with salt and pepper. When the pot is hot, brown the shanks in batches until well browned on one side only, 5 minutes per batch. Transfer the shanks to a plate. Press **CANCEL**. (Alternatively, broil the oiled and seasoned meat on a foil-lined baking sheet, turning once, until browned all over, 10 minutes.)

2   Select **SAUTÉ** and adjust to **NORMAL/MEDIUM** heat. Add the remaining 1 tablespoon oil and when it is hot, add the onion, carrot, celery, thyme, and baking soda. Cook, stirring occasionally, until the vegetables are tender, 4 minutes. Add the garlic and tomato paste and cook until the tomato paste begins to brown and the garlic is fragrant, 45 seconds. Add the wine and cook until some of the alcohol has burned off, 1 minute. Press **CANCEL**.

3   Add the broth and tomatoes to the pot and stir to combine. Return the veal shanks and any accumulated juices to the pot. Lock on the lid, select the **PRESSURE COOK** function, and adjust to **HIGH** pressure for 45 minutes. Make sure the steam valve is in the "Sealing" position and that the "Keep Warm" button is off.

4   When the cooking time is up, let the pressure come down naturally, about 20 minutes. With a spatula, carefully transfer the shanks to a large serving bowl or platter; leave the butcher's twine on the shanks. Cover loosely with foil.

5   Select **SAUTÉ** and adjust to **NORMAL/MEDIUM** heat. When the liquid comes to a simmer, the fat will pool on the top around the edges of the pot. Spoon off the fat and discard.

6   In a small bowl, combine the butter and flour and stir until smooth. Gradually whisk the flour mixture into the cooking liquid and simmer, whisking frequently, until thickened and bubbling, 5 minutes. Press **CANCEL**. Pour the sauce over the shanks and serve.

The osso buco and sauce can be stored in an airtight container for up to 5 days. Reheat gently before serving.

CHICAGO-STYLE ITALIAN BEEF SANDWICHES

Serves 6   Active time: 15 minutes   Total time: 1 hour 30 minutes

These Italian-American sandwiches are stacked high with sliced beef, pepperoncini-spiked jus, and giardiniera pickles, so you'll need sturdy rolls to hold in all the goodness. Delis in Chicago use a spiral meat slicer to get wafer-thin slices of meat. At home, you can either slice the roast with a sharp carving knife into thin slices (best with bottom or rump roast) or shred the meat with two forks (if using chuck roast).

1	(2½-pound) well-marbled beef chuck roast, bottom round roast, or rump roast
1	tablespoon olive oil
1	teaspoon granulated garlic
	Salt and pepper
1½	cups Homemade Beef Broth (page 199) or low-sodium store-bought broth
1	small yellow onion, halved lengthwise and sliced through the root end
½	cup pickled pepperoncini peppers, sliced
3	medium garlic cloves, thinly sliced
1	tablespoon tomato paste
2	teaspoons dried Italian seasoning
6	crusty hoagie or sub sandwich rolls, split lengthwise
1	cup chopped Giardiniera (page 46) or store-bought Italian pickled vegetables

1 Select **SAUTÉ** and adjust to **MORE/HIGH** heat. Brush the roast with the oil and sprinkle with the granulated garlic and a generous amount of salt and pepper. When the pot is hot, add the beef and cook until well browned all over, 8 minutes. Press **CANCEL**.

2 Add the broth, onion, pepperoncini, garlic, tomato paste, and Italian seasoning to the pot and stir to combine. Lock on the lid, select the **PRESSURE COOK** function, and adjust to **HIGH** pressure for 1 hour 20 minutes. Make sure the steam valve is in the "Sealing" position and that the "Keep Warm" button is off.

3 When the cooking time is up, let the pressure come down naturally, about 20 minutes. Transfer the roast to a cutting board and tent with foil. Select **SAUTÉ** and adjust to **MORE/HIGH** heat. Simmer the cooking liquid, uncovered, until reduced slightly, 10 minutes. Spoon off the liquid fat floating on top of the liquid and discard.

4 Thinly slice the roast with a sharp carving knife or slice the meat into thick slices and shred it with two forks (see Headnote). Mound the beef on the rolls, spoon some of the reduced cooking liquid over the top, and top with the giardiniera.

The beef and its cooking liquid can be stored in an airtight container for up to 5 days. Reheat gently before serving.

VENETIAN SPICED LAMB AND RICE

ONE POT

> **Serves 4 to 6** | **Active time: 30 minutes** | **Total time: 1 hour 20 minutes**

This hearty lamb dish features the subtle flavors of cinnamon and cloves, ingredients that were stock and trade for wealthy Venetian traders until the sixteenth century. The use of such spices in savory meat dishes is still a hallmark of Venetian cuisine and adds warm, comforting savor to one-pot meals like this one.

1¾	pounds leg of lamb, fat and silver skin trimmed, cut into 1-inch cubes
	Salt and pepper
2	tablespoons olive oil
1	medium yellow onion, chopped
1	medium carrot, chopped
¼	cup dry white wine
2	cups Homemade Beef or Chicken Broth (page 199 or 198) or low-sodium store-bought broth
1½	cups boxed or canned diced tomatoes in puree
2	cinnamon sticks
6	whole cloves
1	cup Arborio rice
½	cup grated Parmesan cheese
2	tablespoons unsalted butter
2	tablespoons finely chopped fresh Italian parsley

1 Select **SAUTÉ** and adjust to **MORE/HIGH** heat. Toss the lamb chunks with the oil and season generously with salt and pepper. When the pot is hot, add one-third of the meat to the pot and cook, stirring occasionally, until browned, 6 minutes. Transfer the meat to a plate and repeat with the remaining meat in two more batches. (Alternatively, broil the oiled and seasoned meat on a foil-lined baking sheet, stirring once, until browned all over, 10 minutes.)

2 Return all the lamb and any accumulated juices from the plate to the pot. Add the onion and carrot and cook, stirring frequently, until tender, 4 minutes. Add the wine and cook until some of the alcohol burns off, 1 minute. Press **CANCEL**.

3 Add the broth, tomatoes, cinnamon, and cloves and stir to combine. (Do not add the rice at this time.) Lock on the lid, select the **PRESSURE COOK** function, and adjust to **HIGH** pressure for 15 minutes. Make sure the steam valve is in the "Sealing" position and that the "Keep Warm" button is off.

4 When the cooking time is up, quick-release the pressure. Unlock the lid and stir the rice into the lamb mixture. Lock on the lid, select the **PRESSURE COOK** function, and adjust to **HIGH** pressure for 8 minutes. Make sure the valve is in the "Sealing" position and that the "Keep Warm" button is off.

5 When the cooking time is up, let the pressure come down naturally for 10 minutes and then quick-release the remaining pressure. Discard the cinnamon stick and cloves (if you can find them). Stir in half the cheese and the butter and season with salt and pepper. Serve sprinkled with the remaining cheese and the parsley.

BRAISED LAMB SHANKS WITH OLIVES AND ROSEMARY

Serves 4   Active time: 20 minutes   Total time: 1 hour 25 minutes

Look for small lamb shanks (12 ounces to 1 pound each) so you can brown them in the Instant Pot. If you can only find large shanks (1½ pounds each or larger), buy just two and have your butcher saw them in half crosswise (osso buco–style) so they'll fit in the pot. Serve with roasted potatoes or polenta.

4   small (12- to 16-ounce) lamb shanks

2   tablespoons olive oil

Salt and pepper

1   large yellow onion, halved lengthwise and sliced through the root end

1   tablespoon coarsely chopped fresh rosemary, plus 2 sprigs

6   anchovies

12   garlic cloves, peeled and left whole

¼   cup dry red wine

¾   cup Homemade Beef or Chicken Broth (page 199 or 198) or low-sodium store-bought broth

½   cup oil-cured olives, pitted

2   bay leaves

1½   tablespoons cornstarch

1 Select **SAUTÉ** and adjust to **MORE/HIGH** heat. Brush the lamb shanks with 1 tablespoon of the oil and season generously with salt and pepper. When the pot is hot, brown the shanks in batches until browned all over, 8 minutes each batch. (Alternatively, broil the oiled and seasoned shanks on a foil-lined baking sheet 6 inches from the broiling element until browned all over, 10 minutes.) Remove the shanks from the pot and set aside.

2 Add the remaining 1 tablespoon oil to the pot. When the oil is hot, add the onion, rosemary, and anchovies and cook, stirring frequently, until the onion is tender, 4 minutes. Add the garlic cloves and cook for 2 minutes, stirring frequently. Add the wine and cook for 1 minute, scraping up any browned bits from the bottom of the pot. Press **CANCEL**.

3 Add the lamb shanks, broth, olives, and bay leaves to the pot. Lock on the lid, select the **PRESSURE COOK** function, and adjust to **HIGH** pressure for 45 minutes. Make sure the steam valve is in the "Sealing" position and that the "Keep Warm" button is off.

4 When the cooking time is up, let the pressure come down naturally for 15 minutes and then quick-release the remaining pressure. Transfer the lamb shanks to a large serving bowl and cover loosely with foil. Discard the rosemary sprigs and bay leaves.

5 Select **SAUTÉ** and adjust to **MORE/HIGH** heat. When the liquid comes to a simmer, liquid fat will pool on the top around the edges of the pot. Spoon off the fat and discard it. In a small bowl, combine the cornstarch with 1½ tablespoons cold water and stir until smooth. Add to the pot and simmer until the sauce is thickened and bubbling, 3 minutes. Press **CANCEL**. Season the sauce with salt and pepper. Pour the sauce over the lamb and serve.

The lamb shanks and sauce can be stored in an airtight container for up to 5 days. Reheat gently before serving.

MEATBALL SLIDERS

Makes 12; serves 4   Active time: 15 minutes   Total time: 40 minutes

These little beef-and-pork meatballs cook in just 5 minutes in the Instant Pot. They're smothered in mozzarella at the end of cooking and left to stand for just a minute for maximum stretchy cheese goodness. The meatballs can be made and held on the "Keep Warm" function for hours, so they're an ideal treat for game days.

1   slice white sandwich bread, crusts removed

3   tablespoons plain yogurt or half-and-half

8   ounces ground beef chuck

4   ounces ground pork

1   egg yolk

1   small shallot, finely chopped (about 2 tablespoons)

1   teaspoon dried oregano

1   teaspoon fennel seeds

1   teaspoon granulated garlic

½   teaspoon salt

½   teaspoon pepper

3   cups Homemade Marinara Sauce (page 192) or jarred marinara sauce

½   cup Homemade Beef Broth (page 199) or low-sodium store-bought broth

1   cup shredded part-skim mozzarella cheese

1   cup fresh basil leaves

12 slider buns, toasted

1 Tear the bread into small pieces and combine in a large bowl with the yogurt. Mash the mixture with a fork until smooth. Add the beef, pork, egg yolk, shallot, oregano, fennel, granulated garlic, salt, and pepper and blend thoroughly with your hands or a wooden spoon. Form the mixture into 12 meatballs, about 2 tablespoons each, rolling them between your palms to compact them slightly.

2 Pour the marinara sauce and beef broth into the pot, add the meatballs, and lock on the lid. Select the **PRESSURE COOK** function and adjust to **HIGH** pressure for 5 minutes. When the cooking time is done, let the pressure come down naturally for 10 minutes and then quick-release the remaining pressure.

3 Sprinkle the cheese over the top of the meatballs and cover with a metal or glass lid for 5 minutes to allow the cheese to melt.

4 Stack the basil leaves, roll them up tightly like a sleeping bag, and slice them thinly crosswise to create thin ribbons.

5 Serve the meatballs and sauce on the buns, sprinkling with the basil before adding the top half. Pour the sauce into ramekins and serve it on the side for dipping.

The meatballs and sauce can be stored in an airtight container for up to 5 days. Reheat gently before serving.

VEGETABLES

Of course the Instant Pot is great at cooking soups, big roasts, and hearty pasta-and-sauce meals . . . but don't forget your veggies! As you'll see in this chapter, there are tons of ways to use the Instant Pot to make quick, delicious vegetable side dishes (hello, Truffled Celery Root Mashers and Tomato-Braised Green Beans!), plus a few vegetable entrées like eggplant Parmesan and stuffed artichokes.

Cooking in the Instant Pot is remarkably fast, but on the other side of the coin, it can overcook things just as fast. That's why it's key to follow the recipes carefully, mind whether the recipe uses HIGH or LOW pressure, and make sure to cut the vegetables to uniform size so they cook evenly.

You'll be quick-releasing the steam to stop the cooking quickly in many of these vegetable recipes. Be careful when you switch the vent to "Venting": Use a spoon with a long handle to move the vent, and vent beneath a kitchen hood if possible; you might also want to drape a kitchen towel loosely over the vent to disperse the steam a little so it isn't directed straight at your kitchen wall.

CAULIFLOWER WITH GARLIC-ANCHOVY SAUCE

Serves 4 | Active time: 10 minutes | Total time: 30 minutes

Cauliflower, anchovies, and garlic are a flavor match made in heaven, or Southern Italy in this case. Using a whole head of garlic in this dish may seem like a lot, but the cloves become mild and creamy (think roasted garlic) when steamed with the cauliflower. The anchovies add salty umami and don't taste at all fishy once they melt into the oil, but you can substitute chopped Kalamata olives if you like.

1	medium (2-pound) cauliflower
1	large garlic head
⅓	cup extra-virgin olive oil
12	anchovies
1	teaspoon finely grated lemon zest
2	tablespoons fresh lemon juice
	Salt and pepper

1 Remove the outer leaves and stalk from the cauliflower and discard. Break the cauliflower into large (3-inch-wide) florets. Break the garlic head into individual cloves; discard the papery outer skins but leave the peels on the individual cloves.

2 Place a steamer basket in the pot and pour in 1½ cups cold water. Place the garlic cloves in the steamer and top with the cauliflower florets. Lock on the lid, select the **PRESSURE COOK** function, and adjust to **HIGH** pressure for 1 minute. Make sure the steam valve is in the "Sealing" position and that the "Keep Warm" button is off.

3 When the cooking time is up, quick-release the pressure. Transfer the cauliflower to a serving dish, cutting up the largest florets into large bite-size pieces. Squeeze the roasted garlic cloves from their skins into a bowl; discard the skins. Chop the garlic.

4 Discard the water in the pot. Dry the pot and return it to the appliance. Place the oil, garlic, and anchovies in the pot. Select **SAUTÉ** and adjust to **MORE/HIGH** heat. Cook, stirring continuously, until the garlic begins to caramelize and the anchovies fall apart, 3 minutes. Press **CANCEL**.

5 Add the lemon zest and lemon juice to the pot and stir to combine. Pour the sauce over the cauliflower, season generously with salt and pepper, and toss gently to combine.

GLAZED CARROTS WITH GREMOLATA

Serves 4 | **Active time: 5 minutes** | **Total time: 15 minutes**

These carrots are "pressure glazed"—no liquid is added, and just a smidge of baking soda is mixed in to encourage them to caramelize. It's a method I adapted from the excellent cookbook *Modernist Cuisine* by Nathan Myhrvold, Chris Young, and Maxime Bilet. Buy medium carrots with the greens still attached—they'll be sweet and tender, and the tops are used in the *gremolata* garnish.

2   **bunches medium to large carrots with tops (about 2 pounds total)**

2   **tablespoons unsalted butter**

1½   **teaspoons brown sugar**

½   **teaspoon baking soda**

     Salt and pepper

¼   **cup loosely packed fresh basil leaves**

1½   **teaspoons finely grated lemon zest**

1   **small garlic clove, minced**

1   **tablespoon white wine vinegar**

1   Cut the tops off the carrots; set aside ¼ cup of the best-looking leaves and discard the remainder. Peel the carrots and cut them crosswise on an angle into ¾- to 1-inch-thick slices.

2   Place the butter in the pot, select **SAUTÉ**, and adjust to **NORMAL/ MEDIUM** heat. When the butter has melted, add the carrots, brown sugar, baking soda, ½ teaspoon salt, and a few grinds of pepper. Press **CANCEL**. Lock on the lid, select the **PRESSURE COOK** function, and adjust to **HIGH** pressure for 1 minute. Make sure the steam valve is in the "Sealing" position and that the "Keep Warm" button is off.

3   While the carrots are cooking, mound the reserved carrot tops, the basil, lemon zest, and garlic clove on a cutting board and chop until everything is finely chopped and combined.

4   When the cooking time is up, quick-release the pressure. Transfer the carrots and juices from the pot to a serving bowl and sprinkle with the vinegar and the gremolata.

QUICK EGGPLANT PARMESAN

Serves 2 as an entrée or 4 as a side dish   Active time: 10 minutes   Total time: 35 minutes

Calling all eggplant lovers! This streamlined version of the gooey Italian restaurant fave is lighter, faster, and every bit as satisfying. The eggplant halves become perfectly tender in just 5 minutes in the Instant Pot and are then topped with an herby bread crumb mixture and broiled briefly for a crunchy topping—no frying required!

1   medium (1-pound) eggplant, halved lengthwise, stem end discarded

3½ tablespoons olive oil

    Salt and pepper

1¼ cups Homemade Marinara (page 192) or jarred chunky marinara sauce, warmed

2   ounces part-skim mozzarella, cut into ¼-inch-thick slices

1   cup fresh bread crumbs (from 1 slice sturdy white sandwich bread)

3   tablespoons chopped fresh basil

3   tablespoons finely grated Parmesan cheese

½   teaspoon garlic powder

1 Place a trivet with handles in the pot and add 1½ cups water. Score the cut side of the eggplant flesh with a crosshatch pattern (do not cut through the skin). Brush with 1½ tablespoons of the oil and season with salt and pepper. Place the eggplant cut-side up on the trivet. Carefully spoon ½ cup of the marinara onto the cut side of the eggplant, leaving a ¼-inch border all around the edges of the eggplant. Place the mozzarella slices on top, making sure none of the cheese is hanging over the sides.

2 Lock on the lid, select the **PRESSURE COOK** function, and adjust to **HIGH** pressure for 5 minutes. Make sure the steam valve is in the "Sealing" position and that the "Keep Warm" button is off.

3 While the eggplant cooks, preheat the broiler and adjust the oven rack so that it is 6 inches below the broiling element.

4 Spoon the remaining ¾ cup marinara into a small oven-safe baking dish just large enough to hold the eggplant. In a small bowl, mix the bread crumbs with the remaining 2 tablespoons oil, the basil, Parmesan, and garlic powder and stir thoroughly to combine.

5 When the eggplant cooking time is up, quick-release the pressure. Lift the trivet out of the pot and discard the cooking water. Carefully transfer the eggplant with a spatula to the prepared baking dish. Spoon the bread crumb mixture over the eggplant, packing it down lightly. Broil until crispy and browned, 3 minutes.

FENNEL BRAISED IN BALSAMIC VINEGAR AND HONEY

Serves 4   Active time: 15 minutes   Total time: 30 minutes

Fennel is a beloved vegetable all over Italy, from sliced fennel cooked in tomato sauce to chunks of fennel baked in cream with a cloak of Parmesan over the top. My favorite is this simple recipe of fennel wedges braised in a sweet-sour combination of balsamic vinegar and honey. This is the perfect side dish to roasted chicken or pork.

2   large fennel bulbs (about 12 ounces each), stalks and leaves trimmed

2   tablespoons olive oil

1   large shallot, sliced

2   teaspoons chopped fresh rosemary

½   teaspoon baking soda

2   tablespoons aged balsamic vinegar

1   tablespoon honey

Salt and pepper

1 Cut the fennel in half lengthwise and then into 2-inch-thick wedges, making sure there is a bit of the root end attached to each wedge to help keep it together. (Do not cut out the core—it helps hold the wedges together.) You should be able to get 4 to 6 wedges out of each bulb.

2 Put the oil in the pot, select **SAUTÉ**, and adjust to **MORE/HIGH** heat. When the oil is hot, add the shallot, rosemary, and baking soda and cook until tender, 3 minutes. Add the vinegar and honey and press **CANCEL**. Add the fennel and turn the pieces with tongs to coat the wedges in the vinegar mixture. Season with salt and pepper. Lock on the lid, select the **PRESSURE COOK** function, and adjust to **HIGH** pressure for 2 minutes. Make sure the steam valve is in the "Sealing" position and that the "Keep Warm" button is off.

3 When the cooking time is up, quick-release the pressure. Unlock the lid and use a slotted spoon to carefully transfer the fennel wedges to a serving dish. Select **SAUTÉ** and adjust to **MORE/HIGH** heat. Simmer, stirring occasionally, until the liquid has thickened and reduced by half, 2 minutes. Press **CANCEL**. Pour the sauce over the fennel and serve.

BROCCOLI RABE WITH GARLIC AND PEPPADEWS

Serves 4 | Active time: 5 minutes | Total time: 20 minutes

Also known as rapini or broccoli raab, this cousin to broccoli and turnips looks like tall, leafy broccoli. It has a desirable bitterness that's tamed somewhat with moist cooking methods, so it's an ideal candidate for pressure cooking. Substitute Broccolini if you can't find rabe. Peppadew peppers are a mildly spicy pickled pepper available at gourmet groceries; use pickled banana peppers if you can't find Peppadews. This recipe is great as a side dish for roasts or sausage, or try it mounded on top of crostini as an appetizer.

3 tablespoons olive oil

5 garlic cloves, thinly sliced

2 (8-ounce) bunches broccoli rabe, cut into bite-size pieces

¼ cup chopped Peppadew or other pickled peppers

Pinch of red chile flakes

Salt and pepper

1 Put the oil in the pot, select **SAUTÉ**, and adjust to **NORMAL/MEDIUM** heat. When the oil is hot, add the garlic and cook until fragrant but not browned, 45 seconds. Add the broccoli rabe, Peppadews, red chile flakes, a few pinches of salt, and a few grinds of black pepper. Toss to combine. Add ½ cup cold water to the pot and press **CANCEL**.

2 Lock on the lid, select the **PRESSURE COOK** function, and adjust to **HIGH** pressure for 1 minute. Make sure the steam valve is in the "Sealing" position and that the "Keep Warm" button is off.

3 When the cooking time is up, quick-release the pressure. Transfer the vegetables to a platter and spoon a few tablespoons of the cooking liquid over the top.

TOMATO-BRAISED GREEN BEANS

Serves 4   Active time: 10 minutes   Total time: 25 minutes

If you've ever visited Italy, you may have noticed that Italians sometimes cook their vegetables until very soft, what we might consider a little overdone. One of my favorite examples is the dish of flat romano beans or green beans braised in pancetta-studded tomato sauce until they become silky-tender. If you like some shape to your beans, cook them for 3 minutes; for fall-apart-tender beans, go as long as 8 minutes.

1   tablespoon olive oil

¼   cup diced pancetta, from a ½-inch-thick slab

½   medium yellow onion, halved lengthwise and sliced through the root end (about ¾ cup)

2   medium garlic cloves, thinly sliced

¾   cup boxed or canned diced tomatoes in puree

¼   cup Homemade Chicken Broth (page 198) or low-sodium store-bought broth

    Pinch of red chile flakes

    Salt and pepper

1   pound romano or green beans, trimmed and cut into 3-inch lengths

1   tablespoon red wine vinegar

1   Put the oil in the pot, select **SAUTÉ**, and adjust to **NORMAL/MEDIUM** heat. When the oil is hot, add the pancetta and onion and cook, stirring frequently, until the pancetta has rendered its fat and the onion is tender, 4 minutes. Add the garlic and cook until fragrant, 45 seconds. Press **CANCEL**.

2   Add the tomatoes, broth, red chile flakes, ½ teaspoon salt, and a few grinds of black pepper and stir to combine. Add the green beans and toss to coat. Lock on the lid, select the **PRESSURE COOK** function, and adjust to **HIGH** pressure for 3 to 8 minutes (see Headnote). Make sure the steam valve is in the "Sealing" position and that the "Keep Warm" button is off.

3   When the cooking time is up, quick-release the pressure. Add the vinegar to the beans and stir to combine.

WARM POTATO SALAD WITH ARUGULA

Serves 4   Active time: 10 minutes   Total time: 40 minutes

Forget gloppy mayonnaise-laced potato salad—this distinctive Italian-style salad is much lighter and twice as tasty. Buttery fingerling potatoes steam perfectly in the Instant Pot in just 7 minutes, and sprinkling the still-warm potatoes with white wine vinegar infuses them with flavor. Sweet jarred red bell peppers and peppery arugula complete the picture. It's ideal for a picnic, and makes a wonderful side dish for grilled sausages or fish.

1   pound fingerling potatoes, halved lengthwise and cut into 2-inch pieces

Salt

1   small shallot, finely chopped (about ¼ cup)

½   cup jarred roasted red peppers, thinly sliced

2   tablespoons white wine vinegar

3   cups baby arugula, or ½ bunch arugula, chopped

1½   tablespoons olive oil

Pepper

1 Place a steamer basket in the pot and add 1½ cups cold water. Place the potatoes in the steamer and sprinkle with 1 teaspoon salt. Lock on the lid, select the **PRESSURE COOK** function, and adjust to **HIGH** pressure for 7 minutes. Make sure the steam valve is in the "Sealing" position and that the "Keep Warm" button is off.

2 When the cooking time is up, let the pressure come down naturally for 10 minutes and then quick-release the remaining pressure. Transfer the potatoes to a large serving bowl and add the shallot and roasted peppers. Sprinkle the vinegar over the vegetables and let the mixture stand for 5 minutes. Add the arugula and oil and toss gently to combine. Season with salt and black pepper. Serve warm or at room temperature.

The salad, without the arugula, can be stored in an airtight container in the refrigerator for up to 3 days. Bring to room temperature and toss with the arugula just before serving.

SWEET-AND-SOUR DELICATA SQUASH

Serves 4   Active time: 10 minutes   Total time: 35 minutes

Delicata squash have edible peels and a sweet, corn-like flavor that plays nicely with the
Venetian sweet-and-sour combination of caramelized onions, raisins, and vinegar here.
Cooking the delicata under pressure yields moist, tender nuggets of squash in a fraction
of the time it would take on the stove. If you can't find delicata squash,
try this recipe with peeled acorn or butternut squash.

3   tablespoons olive oil

1   medium yellow onion, halved lengthwise and thinly sliced through the root end

2   pounds delicata squash, seeded and cut into 2-inch chunks

½   cup white wine vinegar

½   cup golden raisins

¼   cup Homemade Vegetable or Chicken Broth (page 201 or 198) or low-sodium store-bought broth

  Pinch of red chile flakes

  Salt and pepper

2   tablespoons honey

¼   cup pine nuts, toasted

1 Put the oil in the pot, select **SAUTÉ**, and adjust to **MORE/HIGH** heat. When the oil is hot, add the onion and cook, stirring frequently, until the onion is golden brown, 12 minutes. Press **CANCEL**.

2 Add the squash, vinegar, raisins, broth, red chile flakes, a generous sprinkle of salt, and several grinds of black pepper and stir to combine. Lock on the lid, select the **PRESSURE COOK** function, and adjust to **HIGH** pressure for 6 minutes. Make sure the steam valve is in the "Sealing" position and that the "Keep Warm" button is off.

3 When the cooking time is up, quick-release the pressure. Pour the squash mixture into a large serving bowl. Drizzle the honey over the top and sprinkle with the pine nuts.

SPAGHETTI SQUASH WITH SAGE BROWNED BUTTER

Serves 4 to 6 | Active time: 10 minutes | Total time: 30 minutes

Spaghetti squash requires 1 hour of baking in the oven, but you can put tender, golden strands of squash tossed with toasty browned butter and sage on the table in just 30 minutes with this recipe. The cooked, noodle-like strands of squash can also be served with any of the tomato sauces in this book for a carbohydrate-free "pasta" dish, if you like.

1 medium (2-pound) spaghetti squash, halved lengthwise and seeded

Salt and pepper

3 tablespoons unsalted butter

2 tablespoons chopped fresh sage leaves

1 large garlic clove, thinly sliced

1 Place a trivet in the bottom of the pot and add 1½ cups cold water. Place the squash halves skin-side down in the pot. Season with a generous sprinkling of salt and several grinds of pepper. Lock on the lid, select the **PRESSURE COOK** function, and adjust to **HIGH** pressure for 8 minutes. Make sure the steam valve is in the "Sealing" position and that the "Keep Warm" button is off.

2 When the cooking time is up, quick-release the pressure. Transfer the squash to a cutting board. Drag a fork crosswise over the squash to scrape out the flesh into strands; discard the skins. Place the squash in a large serving bowl and cover with foil.

3 Discard the steaming water, dry out the pot, and return it to the appliance. Put the butter in the pot, select **SAUTÉ**, and adjust to **NORMAL/MEDIUM** heat. When the butter has melted, add the sage and garlic and cook, stirring frequently, until the butter begins to brown and the garlic is just golden brown, 3 minutes. Press **CANCEL**.

4 Pour the butter mixture over the squash and toss to combine

The finished squash dish, with the browned butter, can be stored in an airtight container in the refrigerator for up to 5 days. Reheat gently before serving.

BABY ARTICHOKES WITH LEMON AND THYME

Serves 4   Active time: 25 minutes   Total time: 40 minutes

Braised baby artichokes are a delicacy served as a *contorni*, or side dish,
in Italy to accompany other spring fare like roasted leg of lamb. It takes a bit of
patience to pare the artichokes down to their tender green leaves and hearts,
but they cook in just 4 minutes in the Instant Pot, so the total time
required isn't too long—for artichoke lovers, it's worth every moment.

1	lemon, quartered
10 to 12	baby artichokes (about 2 pounds)
2	tablespoons olive oil
1	small yellow onion, chopped
1	tablespoon chopped fresh thyme
3	medium garlic cloves, chopped
	Salt and pepper
½	cup dry vermouth or dry white wine
1	tablespoon fresh lemon juice
2	tablespoons cold unsalted butter, diced

1 Fill a medium bowl with cold water and the juice of half the lemon. Snap off the leaves from an artichoke until you reach the tender yellow-green leaves at the core, rubbing the cut surfaces with the remaining lemon wedges as you work to prevent browning. With a serrated knife, slice the top quarter off the artichoke and trim off the stem and any tough green leaves still stuck to the base. Cut the artichoke in half lengthwise (or in quarters if the halves are more than 2 inches wide). Scoop out the fuzzy choke in the center of each half with a paring knife, if present (very young artichokes may not have one), and discard. Place the artichoke pieces in the lemon water. Repeat with the remaining artichokes.

2 Put the oil in the pot, select **SAUTÉ**, and adjust to **MORE/HIGH** heat. When the oil is hot, add the onion and thyme and cook, stirring frequently, until tender, 4 minutes. Add the garlic and cook until fragrant, 45 seconds. Drain the artichokes well and add them to the pot with 1 teaspoon salt and several grinds of pepper. Add the vermouth and simmer for 1 minute to boil off some of the alcohol. Press **CANCEL**.

3 Add ½ cup cold water to the pot. Lock on the lid, select the **PRESSURE COOK** function, and adjust to **HIGH** pressure for 4 minutes. Make sure the steam valve is in the "Sealing" position and that the "Keep Warm" button is off.

(recipe continues)

(continued from page 162)

4 When the cooking time is up, quick-release the pressure. Use a slotted spoon to transfer the artichokes to a serving bowl and cover loosely with foil; leave the cooking liquid in the pot. Add the lemon juice to the pot and gradually whisk in the cold butter. Pour the sauce over the artichokes and serve.

The artichokes and sauce, once cooled, can be stored in an airtight container in the refrigerator for up to 3 days. Reheat gently before serving.

TRUFFLED CELERY ROOT MASHERS

Dense celery root and potatoes cook quickly in aromatic steam in the Instant Pot in this recipe to create the silkiest mashed potatoes you've ever had. A little truffle oil and cream add a bit of luxury, but if you'd prefer a less decadent dish, mash the vegetables with some of the steaming liquid instead of cream and skip the truffle oil.

2   garlic cloves, peeled and left whole

4   sprigs fresh thyme

5   whole black peppercorns

1   bay leaf

1   large (1-pound) celery root, peeled and cut into 2-inch chunks

1   medium russet potato, peeled and cut into quarters

4   tablespoons (½ stick) unsalted butter, melted

½   teaspoon freshly grated nutmeg

¼   cup heavy cream, warmed

Salt and pepper

Truffle oil, for garnish

1   Pour 2 cups cold water into the pot and add the garlic, thyme, peppercorns, and bay leaf. Place a steamer basket in the pot and arrange the celery root in it. Top with the potatoes. Lock on the lid, select the **PRESSURE COOK** function, and adjust to **HIGH** pressure for 10 minutes. Make sure the steam valve is in the "Sealing" position and that the "Keep Warm" button is off.

2   When the cooking time is up, let the pressure come down naturally for 10 minutes and then quick-release the remaining pressure. Transfer the celery root, potatoes, and garlic to a bowl and mash with a potato masher until smooth, or run them through a food mill.

3   Add the butter and nutmeg and stir to combine. Gradually add enough of the cream (or steaming liquid; see Headnote) to create a loose, creamy mash. Season with salt and pepper and drizzle with truffle oil.

BUTTERNUT SQUASH WITH ROSEMARY

Serves 4   Active time: 10 minutes   Total time: 30 minutes

Butternut squash contains a large amount of moisture, so there's no need to add any liquid to this recipe in order to bring it up to pressure. The tender squash is lovely when served alongside Turkey Breast with Chestnut Stuffing (page 118) or used as a layer in Creamy Butternut and Kale Lasagna (page 92).

3 tablespoons unsalted butter

1 medium (2-pound) butternut squash, peeled, seeded, and cut into 1½-inch chunks

1 tablespoon coarsely chopped fresh rosemary

½ teaspoon baking soda

Salt and pepper

1 Place the butter in the pot, select **SAUTÉ**, and adjust to **NORMAL/ MEDIUM** heat. When the butter has melted, add the squash, rosemary, baking soda, 1 teaspoon salt, and a few grinds of pepper. Press **CANCEL**.

2 Lock on the lid, select the **PRESSURE COOK** function, and adjust to **HIGH** pressure for 5 minutes. Make sure the steam valve is in the "Sealing" position and that the "Keep Warm" button is off.

3 When the cooking time is up, quick-release the pressure. Pour the squash into a medium serving bowl and serve.

The squash can be refrigerated in an airtight container for up to 5 days. Reheat gently before serving.

🍲 STUFFED ARTICHOKES

Serves 2 to 4 | Active time: 15 minutes | Total time: 40 minutes

The Instant Pot is ideal for steaming artichokes: Just place them on a trivet, add water, and 25 minutes later, you're in business. Stuffing a cheesy, herby bread crumb mixture between the artichoke leaves elevates the thistle to special-occasion status, but it's easy enough to make on a weeknight. You'll be able to fit two large artichokes (about a pound each) or three medium (12 ounces or under) artichokes in the pot. Either way, the recipe will serve four people as a shared side dish, or two as an elegant entrée.

2 cups fresh bread crumbs (from 3 slices sturdy white sandwich bread)

½ cup grated Parmesan cheese

½ cup grated Pecorino Romano cheese

¼ cup chopped prosciutto slices

2 tablespoons chopped fresh basil

3 garlic cloves, finely chopped

Salt and pepper

2 tablespoons olive oil

2 large (1-pound) or 3 medium (12-ounce) artichokes

½ lemon, cut into wedges

½ cup (1 stick) butter, melted, for serving (optional)

1 Place the bread crumbs in a medium sauté pan and cook over medium-low heat, stirring frequently, until golden brown, 4 minutes. Pour into a large bowl and let cool for a few minutes. Add the cheeses, prosciutto, basil, and garlic and stir to combine. Season with salt and pepper. Add the oil and stir to moisten the bread crumbs.

2 With a serrated knife, cut off the top quarter of the artichokes and trim the stems to 1 inch. Rub the cut surfaces with lemon. Separate the leaves to open up the artichokes a little. Push the stuffing down between the leaves, dividing it evenly among the artichokes.

3 Place a trivet in the pot and add 1½ cups cold water. Place the artichokes stem-side down on the trivet. Lock on the lid, select the **PRESSURE COOK** function, and adjust to **HIGH** pressure for 15 minutes. Make sure the steam valve is in the "Sealing" position and that the "Keep Warm" button is off.

4 When the cooking time is up, let the pressure come down naturally for 10 minutes and then quick-release the remaining pressure. To test for doneness, pull a leaf from the center of an artichoke and scrape the tender bottom of the leaf off with your teeth; it should come away easily. If the artichokes need more time, lock the lid back on and cook on **HIGH** pressure for 1 to 3 minutes more. Quick-release the pressure.

5 Use tongs to gently transfer the artichokes to serving plates. Serve with melted butter, if desired.

DESSERTS

The Instant Pot is a great friend to bakers. Sure, you've probably heard about the wonders of Instant Pot cheesecake (there's a stellar amaretto cherry recipe here that is quite simply impossible to stop eating), but there are many more Italian desserts for you to try that let you get your *dolci* on without turning on the oven.

The moist environment of pressure cooking means the following cakes are super-moist. With a few exceptions, they are cooked with the pans uncovered, which allows them to cook quickly with some of the flavorful steam penetrating the cake—a very good thing! The Instant Pot is also great for cooking desserts that would traditionally be cooked in a water bath, like vanilla *budino* custards, caramel chocolate *bonet* (a flan-like cake), and orange-chocolate panettone bread pudding.

To make the following desserts, you'll need an 8-inch springform pan that fits into the Instant Pot pot and a 6-cup metal Bundt pan without handles on the sides (I use one made by Nordic Ware). For the *budino* and individual chocolate-espresso cakes, you'll need 6-ounce porcelain ramekins that hold about ¾ cup liquid with ¼ to ½ inch headroom at the top.

Some writers recommend making a sling out of foil to lift cakes and other desserts out of the Instant Pot. I find that the trivet with handles supplied with most Instant Pot models works just fine—no need to waste foil. The water in the pot will be steaming, of course, so wear oven mitts to lift your goodies out of the pot. To retrieve ramekins from the pot, I use heavy-duty tongs.

CHOCOLATE HAZELNUT CAKE

Serves 8   Active time: 15 minutes   Total time: 1 hour

This is my all-time favorite cake recipe, moist and full of chocolate and hazelnut flavor.
It just happens to be egg- and dairy-free, so it's a great treat for vegans.
Cooking the cake in the moist environment of the Instant Pot yields a remarkably
moist and tender crumb. If you do want the cake to be vegan, use vegan butter sticks
(not whipped vegan butter) such as Earth Balance Buttery Sticks for the frosting,
or use unsalted butter if you don't need a vegan cake.

FOR THE CAKE

- 1⅓ cups all-purpose flour
- 1 cup granulated sugar
- ½ cup unsweetened cocoa powder
- 1 teaspoon baking powder
- 1 teaspoon baking soda
- ½ teaspoon salt
- 1 cup unsweetened soy or almond milk, or cow's milk
- ¼ cup safflower oil or melted coconut oil
- 1 tablespoon Frangelico or other hazelnut liqueur
- ¼ cup finely chopped toasted hazelnuts

FOR THE FROSTING

- ½ cup (1 stick) unsalted butter or vegan butter, at room temperature
- 1¼ cups confectioners' sugar
- ⅓ cup unsweetened cocoa powder
- 1 tablespoon Frangelico or other hazelnut liqueur
- ¼ cup chopped toasted hazelnuts

1 Make the cake: Spray an 8-inch springform pan with cooking spray. Set a trivet in the pot and add 1½ cups hot water. (The trivet should sit high enough in the pot so that the bottom of the cake pan does not touch the water.)

2 Sift the flour, granulated sugar, cocoa powder, baking powder, baking soda, and salt into a large bowl. Set the sifter aside; you will use it again when making the frosting. In a small bowl, whisk together the soy milk, oil, and liqueur. Add the wet ingredients to the dry ingredients and whisk until smooth. Fold in the hazelnuts. Pour the batter into the prepared pan.

3 Place the cake pan, uncovered, on the trivet in the pot. Lock on the lid, select the **PRESSURE COOK** function, and adjust to **HIGH** pressure for 30 minutes. Make sure the steam valve is in the "Sealing" position and that the "Keep Warm" button is off.

4 When the cooking time is up, quick-release the pressure. Insert a wooden skewer into the center of the cake; it should come out clean with a few moist crumbs attached. Remove the pan from the cooker and allow the cake to cool in the pan on a trivet for at least 1 hour.

5 Meanwhile, make the frosting: Place the butter in a large bowl. Sift the confectioners' sugar and cocoa powder over the top and beat on low speed with a handheld mixer until the dry ingredients are incorporated. Add the liqueur and beat on medium speed until fluffy, 1 minute.

6 Remove the sides of the springform pan. Spread the frosting evenly over the cake and sprinkle with the hazelnuts.

The frosted cake can be stored in an airtight container in the refrigerator for up to 5 days.

VANILLA BUDINO WITH BALSAMIC BASIL STRAWBERRIES

Serves 4 | Active time: 30 minutes | Total time: 2 hours

Budino is the Italian word for "pudding," but unlike our stovetop puddings, these custard desserts are cooked in a water bath, more like crème brûlée. The sweet, creamy puddings are paired with sliced strawberries marinated in sugar and balsamic vinegar. The combination may sound odd, but good-quality balsamic vinegar is rich and fruity and cuts the sweetness of the custard perfectly.

1¼ cups heavy cream

½ vanilla bean

5 egg yolks

½ cup plus 2 tablespoons sugar

Salt

1 pint strawberries, hulled and sliced

1 tablespoon balsamic vinegar

2 tablespoons thinly sliced fresh basil leaves

1 Place the cream in a microwave-safe measuring cup or small saucepan. Split the vanilla bean lengthwise with a paring knife. Scrape out the seeds and add them to the cream; add the pod as well. Microwave on high for 2 minutes or heat the saucepan over medium-low heat until the cream is hot to the touch, 8 minutes. Let the mixture stand at room temperature for 5 minutes. Remove and discard the vanilla bean pod or reserve it for another use.

2 In a mixing bowl with a spout, whisk together the egg yolks, ½ cup of the sugar, and a pinch of salt until thick, 2 minutes. Gradually whisk the cream into the egg mixture.

3 Place a trivet in the base of the pot and add 1½ cups cold water. Pour the cream mixture into four medium (6-ounce) oven-safe ramekins. Cover each ramekin tightly with foil. Place the ramekins on the trivet; you will need to stack one ramekin on top of the others so they all fit in the appliance. Lock on the lid, select the **PRESSURE COOK** function, and adjust to **HIGH** pressure for 6 minutes. Make sure the steam valve is in the "Sealing" position and that the "Keep Warm" button is off.

4 When the cooking time is up, let the pressure release naturally, about 10 minutes. Blot the foil with paper towels to remove excess moisture. Remove the ramekins from the appliance with tongs. The custards are done when a paring knife comes out clean when inserted into the center of the custard. Test both the custard stacked on top and one from the bottom layer for doneness. If the top ramekin is not cooked, place it on the trivet,

cover the pot with a regular lid, and let it sit for 5 minutes with the power off; the residual heat will finish cooking the custard. Unwrap the custards and refrigerate them until completely cooled, at least 1 hour.

5 Five minutes before serving, in a large bowl, toss the berries, the remaining 2 tablespoons sugar, and the vinegar. Let stand at room temperature for 5 minutes. Immediately before serving, stir the basil into the berry mixture and spoon it over the chilled custards.

Once cool, the custards can be tightly wrapped with plastic and stored in the refrigerator for up to 4 days.

CASSATA

Cassata is the second most iconic Sicilian dessert after cannoli. Like cannoli, this dessert includes citrus-infused ricotta filling, but here it serves as a filling for orange sponge cake. The cake is finished with an easy whipped cream icing and decorated with pistachios. It's impressive looking, but it's strictly beginner-level baking, especially since the orange-scented cake is steam-baked in the Instant Pot, which practically guarantees a moist crumb.

FOR THE CAKE

- 2 cups all-purpose flour
- 1 cup granulated sugar
- 1 teaspoon baking powder
- 1 teaspoon baking soda
- ½ teaspoon salt
- ¾ cup milk
- ¼ cup safflower oil or melted coconut oil
- 2 teaspoons finely grated orange zest
- ¼ cup fresh orange juice
- 2 teaspoons vanilla extract

FOR THE FILLING AND WHIPPED CREAM

- 2 cups Homemade Ricotta (page 194) or store-bought ricotta (14 ounces)
- 1 cup confectioners' sugar
- ½ cup finely chopped candied orange zest
- 1 teaspoon vanilla
- 1 cup very cold heavy cream
- ½ cup finely chopped pistachios

1. Make the cake: Spray an 8-inch springform pan with cooking spray. Set a trivet with handles in the pot and add 1½ cups hot water. (The trivet should sit high enough so that the bottom of the cake pan won't touch the water.)

2. In a large bowl, whisk together the flour, granulated sugar, baking powder, baking soda, and salt until well combined. In a measuring cup, whisk together the milk, oil, orange zest, orange juice, and vanilla. Add the wet ingredients to the dry ingredients and stir with a rubber spatula until combined. Pour the batter into the prepared pan.

3. Place the cake pan, uncovered, on the trivet in the pot. Lock on the lid, select the **PRESSURE COOK** function, and adjust to **HIGH** pressure for 30 minutes. Make sure the steam valve is in the "Sealing" position and that the "Keep Warm" button is off.

4. When the cooking time is up, quick-release the pressure. Insert a wooden skewer into the center of the cake; it should come out clean with a few moist crumbs attached. Remove the pan from the pot and allow the cake to cool in the pan on a trivet for at least 1 hour.

5. Meanwhile, make the filling and whipped cream: In the bowl of a stand mixer fitted with the paddle attachment, combine the ricotta, ½ cup of the confectioners' sugar, ¼ cup of the candied orange, and the vanilla and beat until fluffy, 2 minutes. Set aside.

6. Remove the pan sides and slide a spatula under the cake to release it from the pan base. Use a serrated knife to cut the cake in half horizontally to make two layers. Place the bottom cake layer on a serving platter. Spread all the ricotta mixture over the bottom cake layer. Place the second cake layer on top of the ricotta.

(recipe continues)

(continued from page 177)

7 Put the cream in a large bowl and sift the remaining ½ cup confectioners' sugar over the cream. Beat until the cream holds stiff peaks, 2 minutes.

8 With an offset spatula, spread the whipped cream evenly over the top and sides of the cake. Gently press the pistachios onto the sides of the cake. Sprinkle the remaining ¼ cup candied orange on the top of the cake. Refrigerate for at least 10 minutes and up to 4 hours before serving.

The cake, without the filling and frosting, can be made up to 1 day ahead. Cool completely in the pan, wrap with foil, and store at room temperature.

CHOCOLATE-AMARETTI STEAMED PUDDING

Serves 6 | Active time: 20 minutes | Total time: 50 minutes, plus overnight chilling

My favorite Italian dessert is the little-known chocolate-almond flan-like confection called *bonet*. The dessert is studded with little bits of *amaretti* cookies. If you can't find *amaretti*, it's fine to substitute almond biscotti or another almond-flavored cookie. The bottom of the baking dish is coated with caramelized sugar; once unmolded, the caramel melts over the cake to produce a bittersweet sauce. Don't be tempted to skip the overnight refrigeration in this recipe; the moisture from the custard helps to dissolve most of the hard caramel in the bottom of the pan.

3 ounces amaretti or other almond cookies

1⅓ cups whole milk

2 tablespoons amaretto liqueur

⅔ cup plus 2 tablespoons sugar

3 large eggs

¼ cup unsweetened cocoa powder

1 cup very cold heavy cream

½ teaspoon vanilla extract

1 Pulse the cookies in a food processor or crush them with a rolling pin in a zip-top bag until the largest pieces are no bigger than a garbanzo bean. Place the cookie crumbs, milk, and liqueur in a medium bowl and set aside to soften while preparing the other ingredients.

2 Spray a 6-cup metal Bundt pan with cooking spray. Place ⅓ cup of the sugar in a small saucepan. Sprinkle with 3 tablespoons cold water; do not stir the sugar, as any stray crystals on the side of the pan can cause the entire pot of caramel to crystallize. Place the pot over medium-high heat and cook until the sugar has melted, 1½ minutes. Increase the heat to medium-high and cook, swirling the pan occasionally to evenly distribute the caramelized parts, until the mixture is the color of a new copper penny, about 3 minutes. Immediately remove the pan from the heat. Carefully pour the syrup into the bottom of the prepared cake pan and tilt the pan to evenly coat.

3 In a large bowl, whisk together the eggs and ⅓ cup of the sugar until the sugar has dissolved and the mixture is thick, 2 minutes. Sift the cocoa over the mixture and stir to moisten. With a rubber spatula, scrape down the sides of the bowl and fold the cookie-milk mixture into the egg mixture. Pour the batter into the prepared pan. Place the uncovered pan on a trivet with handles.

(recipe continues)

(*continued from page 179*)

4 Pour 1½ cups cold water into the pot. Carefully lower the pan-trivet setup into the pot. Lock on the lid, select the **PRESSURE COOK** function, and adjust to **HIGH** pressure for 10 minutes. Make sure the steam valve is in the "Sealing" position and that the "Keep Warm" button is off.

5 When the cooking time is up, let the pressure come down naturally for 10 minutes and then quick-release the remaining pressure. Insert a butter knife into the center of the cake; it should come out clean with a few moist crumbs attached.

6 Cover the cake in the pan with plastic and refrigerate for at least 8 hours and up to 3 days. Uncover the cake and run a knife around the edges to loosen. Place a serving plate on top of the cake pan and invert the pan and plate together. Let the cake with the pan on top sit for a few minutes to allow the caramel to fall over the cake. Remove the cake pan; there will be some caramel still stuck to the bottom of the pan; this is expected. (Soak the pan with hot water to remove stuck-on caramel.)

7 In a medium bowl, whip the cream with the remaining 2 tablespoons sugar and the vanilla until it holds soft peaks. Serve slices of the cake topped with the whipped cream.

MOLTEN ESPRESSO-CHOCOLATE CAKES

Serves 4   Active time: 20 minutes   Total time: 40 minutes

These little cakes must be served immediately once they're done cooking for the full molten-chocolate-center effect, but the batter can be made up to 3 hours in advance, so you could prep them pre-dinner party and pop them into the Instant Pot moments before serving. Garnish the cakes with whipped cream and raspberries, or serve with vanilla gelato.

7   ounces 70% dark chocolate, broken into pieces

6   tablespoons (¾ stick) unsalted butter, cut into pieces

1   tablespoon espresso powder (or decaffeinated espresso powder)

3   large eggs, separated

     Pinch of salt

¼   cup plus 1 tablespoon sugar

1   teaspoon vanilla extract

1. Put 1½ cups hot water in the pot. Select **SAUTÉ** and adjust to **MORE/HIGH** heat. Set a metal bowl over the top of the appliance to make a double boiler. Add the chocolate, butter, and espresso powder to the bowl. Cook, stirring occasionally, until smooth, 5 minutes. Press **CANCEL** whenever the water comes to a simmer. Remove the bowl from the top of the appliance, wipe the bottom of the bowl with a towel, and let the mixture cool for 5 minutes. Leave the water in the pot.

2. Meanwhile, in a medium bowl, combine the egg whites with the salt. Whip with a handheld mixer until the egg whites hold soft peaks. Sprinkle 1 tablespoon of the sugar over the egg whites and continue to beat until the egg whites hold stiff peaks. Set aside.

3. In a large bowl, beat the egg yolks with the remaining ¼ cup sugar until thick and light, 1 minute. Fold the melted chocolate mixture into the egg yolk mixture with a rubber spatula. Add the vanilla and stir to combine. Fold the egg whites into the chocolate mixture in three additions, stopping when there are no longer streaks of egg white in the batter.

4. Spray four 6-ounce oven-safe ramekins with cooking spray and set a trivet in the bottom of the pot. Spoon the batter into the ramekins.

5. Place the ramekins on the trivet; you will need to stack one ramekin on top of the others so they all fit. Lock on the lid, select the **PRESSURE COOK** function, and adjust to **HIGH** pressure for 8 minutes. Make sure the steam valve is in the "Sealing" position and that the "Keep Warm" button is off.

6. When the cooking time is up, quick-release the pressure. Immediately remove the ramekins from the appliance using tongs. You can serve the cakes in the ramekins, or invert them onto plates for a fancier presentation. To invert the cakes onto plates, run a paring knife around the edges of the cakes. Wrap a dry kitchen towel around the edges of each ramekin, place a dessert plate over the top, and invert the plate and ramekin together to release the cake onto the plate. Serve immediately.

The batter-filled ramekins can be refrigerated for up to 3 hours before baking.

CHOCOLATE AND ORANGE PANETTONE BREAD PUDDING

Serves 6   **Active time: 10 minutes**   **Total time: 50 minutes**

Panettone is an enriched raisin bread that is given as a gift around Christmastime in Italy. The loaves are usually quite large and the leftovers go stale quickly, thus the long list of recipes that use leftover panettone, including ice cream cakes and bread puddings like this one. Use raisin challah or brioche during other times of the year when panettone isn't generally available. I like to serve wedges of this dessert with a scoop of orange or chocolate gelato to echo the flavors in the bread pudding.

1   tablespoon unsalted butter, at room temperature, for the pan

½   cup sugar

3   large eggs

1½   cups whole milk

1   tablespoon finely grated orange zest

2   tablespoons orange liqueur, such as Grand Marnier

8   ounces panettone or raisin challah, cut into 1-inch cubes (about 5½ cups)

2   ounces dark chocolate, chopped (about ⅓ cup)

1   Butter an 8-inch round metal baking pan that will fit in the pot. Set a trivet with handles in the pot and add 1½ cups cold water.

2   In a medium bowl, whisk together the sugar and eggs until pale yellow, 1 minute. Add the milk, orange zest, and orange liqueur and whisk to combine.

3   Spread half the bread cubes in the prepared baking pan. Pour half the milk mixture evenly over the bread cubes and press down so the bread absorbs the custard. Sprinkle with half the chocolate.

4   Put the remaining bread cubes in the baking pan in an even layer and pour the remaining custard over the top. Press down gently to moisten all the bread cubes. Sprinkle the remaining chocolate over the top. Set the baking pan, uncovered, in the pot on the trivet. Lock on the lid, select the **PRESSURE COOK** function, and adjust to **HIGH** pressure for 15 minutes. Make sure the steam valve is in the "Sealing" position and that the "Keep Warm" button is off.

(recipe continues)

(continued from page 182)

5 When the cooking time is up, let the pressure come down naturally for 10 minutes and then quick-release the remaining pressure. Insert a butter knife into the center of the pudding, it should come out with no liquid custard coating the knife. If the pudding is not done, lock on the lid and cook on **HIGH** pressure for 1 minute more. Quick-release the pressure.

6 Remove the pan from the pot and let the pudding cool for 10 minutes before serving.

The pudding can be tightly wrapped in plastic and stored in the refrigerator for up to 3 days. Reheat in the oven or microwave before serving.

RICOTTA CHEESECAKE WITH AMARETTO CHERRIES

Serves 8   Active time: 30 minutes   Total time: 2 hours

This dessert delivers a trifecta of almond—a silky-smooth amaretto-spiked ricotta filling, an *amaretti* cookie crust, and fresh cherry and amaretto liqueur sauce. Homemade ricotta makes this filling incredibly creamy, but if you're using store-bought cheese, get a good-quality, whole-milk ricotta such as Calabro brand.

FOR THE CRUST

- 3½ ounces amaretti or other almond cookies
- ⅔ cup sliced almonds (2¼ ounces), toasted
- 2½ tablespoons unsalted butter, melted

FOR THE FILLING

- 1 (8-ounce) package cream cheese, at room temperature
- 1 cup Homemade Ricotta (page 194) or store-bought ricotta (7 ounces)
- ⅔ cup sugar
- 2 teaspoons finely grated lemon zest
- 2 tablespoons amaretto liqueur
- 2 large eggs, at room temperature

FOR THE CHERRY TOPPING

- 12 ounces fresh dark sweet cherries, pitted, or frozen pitted cherries
- 3 tablespoons sugar
- 2 tablespoons amaretto liqueur
- 2 teaspoons cornstarch

1 Make the crust: Spray an 8-inch springform pan with cooking spray. Line the bottom of the pan with parchment paper and spray with cooking spray. In a food processor, pulse the cookies and almonds until finely ground. Add the butter and pulse to combine. Pour the crumb mixture into the pan and press the crumbs over the bottom and 1 inch up the sides of the pan. Refrigerate while making the filling.

2 Make the filling: Wipe out the food processor bowl with paper towels. Place the cream cheese, ricotta, sugar, lemon zest, and amaretto in the food processor and process, stopping once to scrape down the sides of the bowl, until well incorporated. Add the eggs one at a time, pulsing to combine. Pour the mixture into the prepared crust. Cover the pan with foil sprayed with cooking spray and tightly crimp the foil around the edges of the pan.

3 Pour 1½ cups cold water into the pot. Place the pan on a trivet with handles and lower it carefully into the pot. Lock on the lid, select the **PRESSURE COOK** function, and adjust to **HIGH** pressure for 35 minutes. Make sure the steam valve is in the "Sealing" position and that the "Keep Warm" button is off.

4 When the cooking time is up, let the pressure come down naturally, about 15 minutes. Blot the foil with paper towels to remove excess moisture. Carefully remove the trivet-cake setup from the pot and remove the foil. The cake will be a little wobbly in the very center, but not completely liquid; it will continue to cook as it stands at room temperature. Let the cake cool at room temperature for 1 hour. Cover and refrigerate for at least 2 hours.

(recipe continues)

(*continued from page 185*)

5 Meanwhile, make the cherry topping: In a small saucepan, combine the cherries, sugar, and amaretto. Bring to a simmer over medium-low heat. Reduce the heat to low and cook, stirring occasionally, until the sugar dissolves and the cherries are fall-apart tender, 10 minutes for fresh cherries, 5 minutes for frozen.

6 In a small bowl, mix the cornstarch with 1 tablespoon cold water. Add to the cherries and simmer, stirring continuously, until thickened and bubbling, 1 minute. Transfer to a bowl and chill until ready to serve.

7 Run a knife around the edges of the pan, unlock the sides of the pan, and remove the springform ring. Transfer the cake on the pan base to a serving plate. Serve with the cherry topping spooned over the top.

The cheesecake in the pan can be wrapped tightly in plastic and stored in the refrigerator for up to 3 days. The sauce can be stored in an airtight container in the refrigerator for up to 5 days. Serve chilled.

AMALFI LIMONCELLO CAKE

Serves 6   Active time: 10 minutes   Total time: 50 minutes, plus cooling time

The picturesque Amalfi coast just south of Napoli is famous for its lemon trees and its liqueur called *limoncello*. The sweet, golden liqueur is served ice-cold at the end of meals, but it makes a lovely addition to cakes, too. It's common to use olive oil as a fat in baking in Italy; be sure to use a mild, buttery-tasting olive oil for the subtlest flavor.

FOR THE CAKE

- 2 cups all-purpose flour
- ⅔ cup granulated sugar
- 2 teaspoons baking powder
- ½ teaspoon baking soda
- ¼ teaspoon salt
- 1 cup full-fat lemon yogurt
- 2 large eggs
- ¼ cup mild olive oil
- ¼ cup limoncello liqueur
- 2 teaspoons lemon zest
- 1½ teaspoons vanilla extract

FOR THE ICING

- 1 cup confectioners' sugar
- 1½ tablespoons fresh lemon juice
- 1 tablespoon limoncello liqueur

1 Make the cake: Spray a 6-cup Bundt pan with cooking spray. Set a trivet with handles in the pot and add 1½ cups hot water.

2 In medium bowl, whisk together the flour, granulated sugar, baking powder, baking soda, and salt. In another medium bowl, whisk together the yogurt, eggs, oil, limoncello, lemon zest, and vanilla.

3 Add the wet ingredients to the dry ingredients and stir with a rubber spatula until just blended with no traces of flour remaining. Scrape the batter into the prepared Bundt pan and smooth the top with a spatula.

4 Place the Bundt pan, uncovered, on the trivet in the pot. Lock on the lid, select the **PRESSURE COOK** function, and adjust to **HIGH** pressure for 30 minutes. Make sure the steam valve is in the "Sealing" position and that the "Keep Warm" button is off.

5 When the cooking time is up, quick-release the pressure. Remove the lid carefully so the condensation on the inside of the lid does not drip back into the pot and onto the cake. Insert a wooden skewer into the center of the cake; it should come out mostly clean with a few moist crumbs attached. Remove the pan from the appliance and let the cake cool in the pan on a trivet for at least 1 hour.

6 Meanwhile, make the icing: Sift the confectioners' sugar into a medium bowl. Add the lemon juice and limoncello and stir until smooth. Invert the cake onto a serving plate and remove the pan. Poke the cake all over with a chopstick or skewer to make channels for the icing to sink into the cake. Slowly pour the icing over the cake.

7 Cut the cake into wedges and serve.

The cake without icing can be tightly wrapped in plastic, or the iced cake covered with a cake dome, and stored in the refrigerator for up to 3 days.

PANTRY

Italian cooks know that home-cooked beans, broths, and tomato sauce are the keys to the kitchen. Homemade staples like these taste better and are often better for you because you can control the quality of the ingredients, without preservatives or excessive amounts of salt. The Instant Pot makes these recipes so easy, there's no excuse not to make them from scratch. And all these staples store well, so you can have your own Italian pantry at your fingertips whenever you need.

HOMEMADE MARINARA

Makes 8 cups Active time: 15 minutes Total time: 1 hour 10 minutes

When tomatoes are in season, I like to make this rich, all-purpose sauce and store it in the freezer for future use. When good, local tomatoes aren't available, this recipe is almost as good using canned tomatoes. San Marzano tomatoes, an heirloom variety that's favored for their big, sweet flavor and meaty texture, are the best canned variety. Cans labeled "DOP" (Protected Designation of Origin) come only from the San Marzano region in Italy, and while costly, they yield incredible sauce. But the term "San Marzano" is also used to refer to tomatoes not necessarily grown in Italy. These tomatoes are usually quite tasty, and cheaper.

2   tablespoons olive oil

1   large yellow onion, finely chopped

1   tablespoon fresh oregano, or 1½ teaspoons dried

½   teaspoon baking soda

6   medium garlic cloves, finely chopped

2   tablespoons tomato paste

½   cup dry red wine (optional)

4   pounds ripe plum tomatoes, peeled and chopped, or 2 (28-ounce) cans whole peeled San Marzano tomatoes, chopped (see Note), with their juices

½   cup Homemade Chicken or Vegetable Broth (page 198 or 201) or low-sodium store-bought broth

2   (6-inch) sprigs fresh basil, plus ½ cup chopped fresh basil leaves

1   (2-inch) Parmesan cheese rind (optional)

Salt and pepper

1 Put the oil in the pot, select **SAUTÉ**, and adjust to **MORE/HIGH** heat. When the oil is hot, add the onion, oregano, and baking soda and cook, stirring frequently, until the vegetables are tender, 4 minutes. Add the garlic and tomato paste and cook, stirring continuously, until the garlic is fragrant, 45 seconds. Add the wine and cook for 1 minute to burn off some of the alcohol. Press **CANCEL**.

2 Add the tomatoes and their juices, broth, basil sprigs, and cheese rind (if using). Add ¾ teaspoon salt and several grinds of pepper. Lock on the lid, select the **PRESSURE COOK** function, and adjust to **HIGH** pressure for 40 minutes. Make sure the steam valve is in the "Sealing" position and that the "Keep Warm" button is off.

3 When the cooking time is up, let the pressure come down naturally for 10 minutes and then quick-release the remaining pressure. Discard the basil stems and cheese rind. Add the chopped basil and season the sauce with salt and pepper. Use immediately, or let the sauce cool completely, uncovered, in the refrigerator and store for later use.

Note: Chopping canned tomatoes can be a messy pain in the neck! To chop canned tomatoes without making a huge mess, simply snip them directly in the can using clean kitchen scissors.

The sauce can be stored in airtight containers in the refrigerator for up to 5 days or in the freezer for up to 3 months.

BASIL PESTO

Makes 1 cup   Active time: 10 minutes   Total time: 10 minutes

Basil pesto is a key ingredient in Pesto Roasted Chicken (page 106) and Octopus, Pesto, and Potato Salad (page 48). It's also an indispensable flavor booster whenever you want to add an Italian flourish to a soup, pasta dish, or vinaigrette.

2   cups packed fresh basil leaves (about 1 ounce)

¼   cup pine nuts or walnuts, toasted

2   medium garlic cloves, chopped

1   tablespoon fresh lemon juice

     Salt

6   tablespoons olive oil

½   cup grated Parmesan cheese

     Pepper

1 In a blender or food processor, combine the basil, pine nuts, garlic, lemon juice, and a big pinch of salt. Pulse briefly to combine. With the machine running, slowly add the oil in a steady stream, stopping as necessary to scrape down the sides with a rubber spatula. Blend or process until smooth.

2 Transfer the basil mixture to a bowl and stir in the cheese. Season with salt and pepper.

The pesto can be stored in an airtight container in the refrigerator for up to 3 days or in the freezer for up to 3 months. Pour a thin layer of olive oil over the pesto to cover before storing. Defrost frozen pesto in the refrigerator.

HOMEMADE RICOTTA

Makes about 2 cups | Active time: 5 minutes | Total time: 40 minutes

Store-bought ricotta can't hold a candle to creamy, rich homemade cheese. You don't need any special equipment, and the **YOGURT** setting on most Instant Pot models gently heats the milk to the perfect temperature, so there's no worrying about scorching the milk on the stove. If you don't have a **YOGURT** setting, heat the milk on **SAUTÉ** on **NORMAL/MEDIUM** heat, stirring occasionally, until a thermometer reaches 190°F before proceeding as directed.

Ricotta is only as good as the milk you use to make it, so buy the best milk you can find and make sure that it isn't ultra-high-temperature (UHT) pasteurized milk. The UHT process changes the proteins in the milk and will prevent it from forming curds.

You can use fresh lemon juice to make the milk coagulate, but I find it easier to add citric acid, which you can find at spice shops or buy online.

The liquid left over in the pot after cheese making is called whey, as in Little Miss Muffet's "curds and whey." It's full of beneficial probiotic organisms, amino acids, vitamins, and minerals, so don't pour it down the drain! You can use it in soups, sauces, and smoothies as a neutral-flavored liquid that adds a big nutritional boost.

8 cups whole milk

⅓ cup fresh lemon juice, or ¾ teaspoon citric acid

¼ teaspoon salt (optional)

1 Pour the milk into the pot and cover with a regular pot lid that fits on top of the Instant Pot. Select the **YOGURT** function and adjust until the digital display reads **BOIL**. When the cooking time is up, remove the lid, being careful not to let any condensation drip back into the pot.

2 Remove the inner pot from the appliance and place it on a trivet. Add the lemon juice or citric acid and stir gently a few times (overzealous stirring will yield cheese with a grainy texture) until you begin to see the milk coagulate—there will be a separation between bright white chunks of curd and thin yellowish liquid whey. This will take about 30 seconds. Stop stirring and let the mixture stand for 5 minutes.

3 Line a a fine-mesh sieve or colander with cheesecloth or a clean, thin cotton-sack towel and set it over a large bowl. Carefully pour the cheese and whey into the colander.

4 For moist, creamy ricotta, let the cheese drain for 5 minutes. For firmer ricotta, allow the cheese to drain for up to 4 hours at room temperature. When the cheese is done draining, stir in the salt (if using). Save the whey for another use (see Headnote). Transfer the cheese to an airtight container and refrigerate.

The ricotta can be stored in an airtight container in the refrigerator for up to 5 days or in the freezer for up to 3 months.

QUICK-SOAKED AND SLOW-SOAKED BEANS

For the recipes in this book that use beans, you'll need plump beans that hold their shape. While I'd love to tell you that you can just throw dried unsoaked beans into the Instant Pot, press a button, and get great results, it's simply not the case. After exhaustive tests, I've found that cooking dry, unsoaked beans in the Instant Pot yields an inconsistent mix of exploded, falling-apart beans and others that are still crunchy.

That's why I recommend soaking dried beans before cooking them, especially when pressure-cooking. A few seconds of forethought will pay off in evenly cooked beans with creamy interiors and intact skins. They take little attention or time, and you'll be rewarded with evenly cooked, plump beans. To finish cooking them, see the recipe for Pressure-Cooked Cannellini or Borlotti Beans (opposite). There are two ways to approach pre-soaking:

OVERNIGHT SOAKING METHOD

To soak the beans "overnight" (or all day, depending on when you plan to cook them), pick over the beans and toss out any rocks or shriveled beans. Rinse the beans well, drain them, and place them in a large bowl. Add enough cold water to cover the beans by 3 inches. Soak the beans for 8 to 12 hours. Drain and rinse the beans before proceeding.

QUICK SOAKING METHOD

To "quick-soak" dried beans in the Instant Pot, pick over the beans and toss out any rocks or shriveled beans. Rinse the beans well, drain them, and place them in the Instant Pot. Add enough cold water to cover the beans by 3 inches. Select SAUTÉ, and adjust to MORE/HIGH heat. As soon as the beans come to a simmer, cook for 2 minutes and then press CANCEL. Remove the pot from the appliance and let the beans stand for 1 hour in the hot water. Drain and rinse the beans before proceeding.

PRESSURE-COOKED CANNELLINI OR BORLOTTI BEANS

Makes 8 to 10 cups | Active time: 10 minutes | Total time: 45 minutes

Home-cooked cannellini and borlotti (aka cranberry) beans are head and shoulders better than any canned beans. Plump and full of flavor, they are a springboard to a plethora of recipes in this book. Since these beans are so versatile and freeze well, I usually make a big batch (2 cups dried beans) at a time and freeze them in zip-top bags with 1½ cups (the yield of a 14-ounce can) in each bag.

When cooking dried beans, refrain from adding any acidic ingredients like tomatoes, wine, or vinegar as they cook; acidity will prevent the beans from tenderizing, no matter how long you cook them. If you'd like to add these ingredients, do so after the beans are tender. Contrary to old lore, adding salt to the pot when cooking dried beans does not make them tough, but it will make them tastier.

Dried beans become tougher and drier the longer they sit on the shelf, so keep in mind that the following cooking time is the median time required for plump but still intact beans.

Cooking the beans on **LOW** pressure and naturally releasing the pressure after cooking helps the beans retain their shape; **HIGH** pressure and quick-release yield mushy beans. You can reduce this recipe by as much as half without adjusting the timing.

4 to 5 **cups soaked and drained borlotti or cannellini beans (from 2 cups dried beans; see opposite page)**

1 medium yellow onion, chopped

1 tablespoon olive oil

1 large garlic clove, peeled and left whole

1 teaspoon salt

1 bay leaf

Prosciutto rind or ham bone (optional)

1. Place the beans, onions, oil, garlic, salt, bay leaf, and prosciutto rind or ham bone (if using) in the pot. Add just enough water to almost come up to the level of the beans; no need to cover them with lots of liquid.

2. Lock on the lid, select the **PRESSURE COOK** function, and adjust to **LOW** pressure for 5 minutes. Make sure the steam valve is in the "Sealing" position and that the "Keep Warm" button is off.

3. When the cooking time is up, let the pressure come down naturally until all the pressure is released, about 10 minutes. Check the beans to make sure they are tender. If they need more cooking, select **SAUTÉ** and adjust to **NORMAL/MEDIUM** heat, cover with a regular pot lid, and simmer gently until done.

4. Drain the beans, place them in a large bowl, and let cool completely, uncovered, in the refrigerator.

The beans can be stored in airtight containers or zip-top bags in the refrigerator for up to 5 days or in the freezer for up to 3 months.

HOMEMADE CHICKEN BROTH

Makes 8½ cups | Active time: 10 minutes | Total time: 2 hours

Pressure cooking chicken bones is the best way to draw out all their collagen and flavor. Use whatever chicken bits are least expensive: Wings, backs, and even drumsticks will yield excellent broth. Browning the chicken by broiling adds additional flavor and a deep golden color to the broth, but this step is optional if you're in a rush.

3 pounds chicken parts
   (wings, backs, drumsticks)

   Salt

1 large yellow onion,
   chopped

2 large carrots, chopped

2 celery ribs, chopped

6 whole black peppercorns

2 sprigs fresh thyme

1 bay leaf

1 Preheat the broiler and adjust the oven rack so that it is 6 inches below the broiling element. Line a rimmed baking sheet with foil and spray with cooking spray. Season the chicken parts generously with salt and arrange them in an even layer on the prepared baking sheet. Broil, turning once, until the chicken is well browned, 15 minutes.

2 Transfer the chicken and any drippings on the baking sheet to the pot. Add 8 cups cold water, the onion, carrots, celery, peppercorns, thyme, and bay leaf to the pot. Lock on the lid, select the **PRESSURE COOK** function, and adjust to **HIGH** pressure for 45 minutes. Make sure the steam valve is in the "Sealing" position and that the "Keep Warm" button is off.

3 When the cooking time is up, let the pressure come down naturally, about 30 minutes. Strain the broth through a fine-mesh strainer into a large bowl; discard the solids. Refrigerate, uncovered, for at least 1 hour, until cooled completely. Spoon off the fat that rises to the top and discard it or reserve for another use. Transfer the broth to airtight containers.

The broth can be stored in airtight containers in the refrigerator for up to 5 days or in the freezer for up to 3 months.

HOMEMADE BEEF BROTH

Makes 8 cups   Active time: 15 minutes   Total time: 2 hours

Beef broth is used in Italian cuisine as the base for soups, meaty braises, and even pasta sauces that feature meat. For the richest-tasting broth, use a mix of meaty bones like oxtails and collagen-rich marrow bones.

3 pounds meaty beef bones

Salt and pepper

1 medium yellow onion, coarsely chopped

1 large carrot, coarsely chopped

2 celery ribs, coarsely chopped

2 tablespoons tomato paste

10 whole black peppercorns

6 sprigs fresh thyme

1 bay leaf

1 Preheat the broiler and adjust the oven rack so that it is 6 inches below the broiling element. Line a rimmed baking sheet with foil and spray with cooking spray. Season the bones generously with salt and pepper and arrange them in a single layer on the prepared baking sheet. Broil until well browned, 6 to 8 minutes. Flip the bones with tongs and broil until browned on second side, 5 minutes more.

2 Transfer the bones and any browned bits and accumulated juices from the baking sheet to the pot. Add 8 cups cold water, the onion, carrot, celery, tomato paste, peppercorns, thyme, and bay leaf to the pot. Lock on the lid, select the **PRESSURE COOK** function, and adjust to **HIGH** pressure for 45 minutes. Make sure the steam valve is in the "Sealing" position and that the "Keep Warm" button is off.

3 When the cooking time is up, let the pressure come down naturally, about 30 minutes. Strain the broth through a fine-mesh sieve into a large bowl; discard the solids. Refrigerate, uncovered, for at least 1 hour, until cooled completely. Spoon off the fat that rises to the top and discard it or reserve it for another use. Transfer the broth to airtight containers.

The broth can be stored in airtight containers in the refrigerator for up to 4 days or in the freezer for up to 3 months.

HOMEMADE SEAFOOD BROTH

Makes 8 cups | Active time: 10 minutes | Total time: 1 hours 40 minutes

Homemade fish broth is a key ingredient for Italian seafood dishes like Ligurian Fish Soup (page 52) and Scallop, Fennel, and Prosecco Risotto (page 96). It's also guaranteed to take your favorite chowder recipe to the next level. Ask your fishmonger for bones from mild, white-fleshed fish like halibut, cod, and trout for this recipe; oilier fish like salmon have too strong a flavor.

3 pounds fish bones from mild, white-fleshed fish (such as halibut, cod, trout, bass)

1 medium yellow onion, chopped

1 large leek, white and light green parts only, halved lengthwise, rinsed well, and chopped

1 cup chopped fennel bulb

2 medium garlic cloves, thinly sliced

10 whole black peppercorns

2 sprigs fresh thyme

1 bay leaf

1 Cut the bones up so they fit into the pot, if necessary. Combine the bones, onion, leek, fennel, garlic, peppercorns, thyme, and bay leaf in the pot. Add 8 cups cold water. Lock on the lid, select the **PRESSURE COOK** function, and adjust to **HIGH** pressure for 30 minutes. Make sure the steam valve is in the "Sealing" position and that the "Keep Warm" button is off.

2 When the cooking time is up, let the pressure come down naturally, about 30 minutes. Strain the broth through a fine-mesh strainer into a large bowl; discard the solids. Refrigerate, uncovered, for at least 1 hour, until cooled completely. Transfer the broth to airtight containers.

The broth can be stored in airtight containers in the refrigerator for up to 3 days or in the freezer for up to 3 months.

HOMEMADE VEGETABLE BROTH

Makes about 8 cups | Active time: 5 minutes | Total time: 1 hour 20 minutes

Homemade vegetable broth is a handy pantry staple that can add savory flavor to soups, one-pot pastas, and other dishes. The combination of vegetables is adaptable—feel free to add leeks, fennel, tomatoes, red bell peppers, or any other vegetables that strike your fancy. Avoid vegetables from the Brassica family, such as cabbage and broccoli, as they'll lend a skunky note. The nutritional yeast adds a rich, savory flavor and golden color, but it's optional.

1 medium yellow onion, chopped

2 carrots, coarsely chopped

2 celery ribs, coarsely chopped

1 leek, halved, rinsed well, and chopped

1 tablespoon tomato paste

1 tablespoon nutritional yeast (optional)

10 whole black peppercorns

2 sprigs fresh thyme

1 bay leaf

1 Place the onion, carrots, celery, leek, tomato paste, nutritional yeast (if using), peppercorns, thyme, and bay leaf in the pot. Add 8 cups cold water. Lock on the lid, select the **PRESSURE COOK** function, and adjust to **HIGH** pressure for 20 minutes. Make sure the steam valve is in the "Sealing" position and that the "Keep Warm" button is off.

2 When the cooking time is up, let the pressure come down naturally, about 30 minutes. Strain the broth through a fine-mesh sieve into a large bowl; discard the solids. Refrigerate, uncovered, for at least 1 hour, until cooled completely. Transfer the broth to airtight containers.

The broth can be stored in airtight containers in the refrigerator for up to 5 days or in the freezer for up to 3 months.

ACKNOWLEDGMENTS

There were many who lent a hand in producing this book. *Mille grazie* to my agent, Jenni Ferrari-Adler, for helping me find a home for my experience and passion for Italian cooking and my enthusiasm for the Instant Pot. Thanks also to Stephanie Fletcher, my editor, who was so encouraging and offered many insightful suggestions. Much appreciation to the image team of photographer Lauren Volo, food stylist Molly Schuster, and prop stylist Martha Bernabe for making my work look so delectable.

A warm ladleful of gratitude to my husband for his support and willing fork, and a deep bow of thanks to the wonderful women who tirelessly helped me test (and retest) the recipes herein. Liz Tarpy's culinary acumen, incredible attention to detail, and hilarious notes were integral to this project; I simply could not have done this without her help. Many thanks also to Danielle Centoni, Rebecca Gagnon, Nicole Kondra, Mora Chatarand, Wendy D'Agostino, and my best friend and pastry expert, Catherine Schutz. Thanks also to Michelina, who repeatedly reminded me, "You made it, you always do." *Molte grazie a tutti voi!*

INDEX

Note: Page references in *italics* indicate photographs.

A

B

C

Also Authorized by Instant Pot®

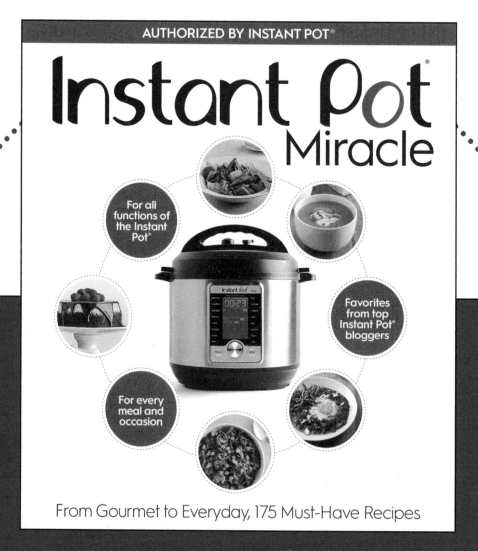

AUTHORIZED BY INSTANT POT®

Instant Pot® Miracle

For all functions of the Instant Pot®

Favorites from top Instant Pot® bloggers

For every meal and occasion

From Gourmet to Everyday, 175 Must-Have Recipes

THE ULTIMATE INSTANT POT® COMPANION

Available where books are sold.

ISBN: 978-1-328-85105-5
$22.99

Houghton Mifflin Harcourt